IN HONOR

I present this book in honor of my two children.
I have cherished both of you since the day you entered my life.
I never take a moment with you for granted.
I love being your Dad.

BIG HUGS

Thank you to all the people who were there for me
at critical points in my journey:

Sion Boney
Ed "Chow" Catto
Phil Cohen
Sharon D'Agostino
Rose Ann Hoffman
Donna Imperato
Shaz Kahng
Lisa Kent
Gwen Korbel
Joyce Myers
Wayne Nelson
Becky and Ray O'Hara
Helayne Spivak
Anne Stroup
Bruce Summers
Dick Thomas
Judy and Brian Welch

And of course, my entire family.

Mascot Books
560 Herndon Parkway #120
Herndon, VA 20170
info@mascotbooks.com

PRBVG0515A

Library of Congress Control Number: 2015900710

ISBN-13: 978-1-63177-028-9

Printed in the United States

www.mascotbooks.com

OUT&
ABOUT
DAD

*My journey as a father
with all its twists, turns,
and a few twirls...*

JIM JOSEPH

WITHOUT GWEN

Gwen Korbel is a very special friend to me. When I think of "unconditional support," I think of Gwen Korbel. It's just who she is.

I've known Gwen for years, both personally and professionally. When we first met, we were working together but over time we became personal friends. After the first day I met her, I donned her with a nickname: Bubbly. Think about it.

Gwen has been nudging me to write this book for a long time. For years she has said to me, "When you get your marketing books done, then you have to write the 'other' book."

This is the "other" book.

Gwen is the one person who convinced me to write my story. Gwen is the one person who convinced me that it's an important story to tell. Gwen is the one person who convinced me that maybe it could help others.

I do what I'm told.

Without Gwen, this book would have never happened.

I believe the children are our future...

THIS IS MY JOURNEY, THIS IS MY STORY

"See, if you look way back there, you can see
the tooth way back there. I can't even touch that tooth way
back there so how can I clean that tooth way back there."

He was the cutest, most articulate four-year-old boy I had ever seen in my life. He had gotten up from his seat at the conference table to rush over to what he thought was a mirror, to show the rest of the people in the room the inside of his mouth.

The moderator had asked the group a question about how they brush their teeth, and he was the first to jump up and answer it, complete with a visual aid.

The little boy was wearing a pair of denim jeans, a green graphic t-shirt, perfectly white sneakers, and a backwards baseball cap. He had turned his cap around so he could get closer to the mirror, which made his big chocolate brown eyes just shine. He was adorable.

He melted my heart and I wanted to pick him up, put him in my pocket, and take him home with me. Cap and all.

What he didn't realize, but his mother did, was that the "mirror" was actually a one-way mirror with a bunch of marketing executives from Johnson & Johnson sitting behind it. When he was opening his mouth into the "mirror," he was actually looking right into our faces. I had a front row seat.

Oh, he kept going, making us all laugh out loud.

He was sticking both his fingers and his toothbrush in his mouth, running them up and down his teeth, talking about each and every tooth and how he tried to brush each one with his toothbrush. Of course his chubby little fingers could barely hold the brush, especially since he was talking with his hands so much!

The scene was a focus group of about eight young kids and their moms, talking about their experiences brushing their teeth. Or rather, not brushing their teeth, which is generally the case since it's so hard for kids that age to reach all around their mouth…they just don't have the manual dexterity it takes to brush thoroughly.

A "focus group" is where marketers bring together a group of consumers to test new ideas, and where a research moderator interviews these consumers to capture their reactions on tape. They basically get to try new stuff and we get to see how they like it.

Enter me, Jim Joseph, a bright-eyed and fresh-faced Assistant Brand Manager in marketing, eager to make my mark on the Reach Toothbrush brand. I was about a year or so into the job after graduating with an MBA from Columbia University.

The year was 1990 and Madonna was in *Vogue*.

I felt like I had my dream job. I was in charge of designing, creating, and launching a brand new toothbrush that would make it easier for kids to brush their teeth. We had figured out that almost all kids' toothbrushes were merely scaled down versions of the adult size; none were specially designed for the clumsy little fingers of a young child.

That night in the focus group we were testing prototypes of a new design that had a thicker, rubberized handle and a specially-angled neck so that a kid's slippery hand could grasp the brush and move it around the teeth in their mouth. It was quite cool.

But nothing compared to that little boy in the turned around baseball cap and the denim jeans. He sparked something in me that I can't really explain. I wanted to have one just like him! Ten of them even!

But looking into his big brown eyes and seeing that wide-open mouth, I had no idea the amount of responsibility that came with having a child. I couldn't even imagine the work that came with being a dad; that part wasn't on my radar yet.

I had been married a couple of years and lived on a quiet street in a precious little town called Yardley in Bucks County, PA. I say it was a quiet street because it was only one block long and had virtually no traffic. But it was constantly bustling with the neighborhood children, which is what I loved most about it.

When I would pull in the driveway coming home from work, I'd often start playing with the little boys next door, or end up talking to the little girls down the street. They started to become like family to me, and they were definitely just like the family that I wanted to eventually have myself.

There were times I'd even take the little boy next door on errands with me, that's how much I loved being around these kids. I wanted to see what it was going to be like to have one of my own.

So when I saw that little boy and all the other kids in the focus group that day, I knew it was time to start thinking about having a family.

I went on to launch that very special toothbrush, The Reach WonderGrip. It quickly became the number one kids' toothbrush in three short months and years later the brand was still selling over fifteen million brushes a year! I had scored my first big win of my career...but I had only just begun!

I knew I was going to be a great marketer for sure, but one day I was also going to be a great dad.

I could just feel it. *One day soon*, I thought to myself, *I'm going to be a dad.* Dad.

It's a word and a concept that carries very personal meaning to each of us, based on our own experience.

For me, I came to vividly understand that fatherhood means responsibility...responsibility for the physical and emotional wellbeing of my children. Sure, having a cute little kid seems like fun and games when you pull into the driveway, but fatherhood is a tremendous responsibility that never stops. Yes it can be exhilarating, but it's also backbreaking at the same time.

Actually, all of the time.

The decision to be a dad is permanent, obviously, but it's not static. Kids don't stay four years old forever. As our children's physical and emotional needs change through the years, fatherhood changes as well.

Three years later I did have a daughter and it was just that...exhilarating. Eighteen months after when I had my son, it was just that again: exhilarating. Along with many crushing and heartbreaking moments along the way.

It's not easy for any parent, but my story is well outside the norm, at least it was when I was raising my kids twenty years ago. While every parent faces their own obstacles, I'm not sure that many faced the same ones that I did at the time.

By today's standards, my story wouldn't be so unusual, but there was a day when I was alone in my journey, with very few other fathers like me. There were certainly no hashtags to rally around.

While I was raising my children as a primary caregiver, I was dealing with issues that few others found themselves tackling. For me, it was a time of great struggle, isolation, and fear, along with a constant balancing act between work and family…one that almost broke me on more than a few occasions.

Along the way, I kept all the bad stuff inside and just focused on raising my children, figuring out how to succeed at my work, and trying to be happy.

"Put your head down and plow ahead."

It's a motto that I've lived my life by, a way of behaving that has served me well through the years. I just don't complain about life, I never have. I put my head down, I plow ahead, and I get things done.

I've often been accused of being overly optimistic as a result, especially at work. I'll take it.

I've also been accused of glossing over the negative. Maybe; I'll take that too.

Even to this day, no one ever looks at me and thinks that perhaps I could be struggling inside. Quite the contrary, most think that my accomplishments have come rather easily, including raising two healthy and happy children into adulthood.

Most people looked at me through the years and assumed I was living an easy life, but that couldn't have been farther from the truth.

Day after day I juggled the demands of parenthood and career, just like many other parents. I rarely missed a day at work, never missed a deadline, and tried to make nearly every school event. I did it at a time when there were very few other fathers doing the same. There were certainly no fathers like me as far as I knew.

When I picked my kids up at night after working all day long, fed them dinner, bathed them, and put them to bed, I never complained about it. Why would I? I'm their dad and that's what I'm supposed to do; that's what I signed up to do. That's what my parents did for me.

I've always had the ability to focus, no matter the situation; I don't moan or talk about it with others. But just because I don't share my struggles doesn't mean they're not there.

Was I too embarrassed to say anything? I don't think that was it.

Was I being a coward? Absolutely not. Not sharing my struggles was how I chose to handle my personal issues and in some ways that's how I was forced to handle them at the time.

Was I afraid to say anything? I think so, but I had my reasons.

When I was growing up, men were expected to date women, find the right girlfriend, get engaged before she gets too restless, get married a year later, and then have children within a designated amount of time. That was *the* plan that we were supposed to follow.

That was how life was *supposed* to work.

Dads were for playtime and for the occasional scolding; moms were the homemakers and social organizers. Dads played catch in the backyard after mowing the lawn, while moms stayed in the house cooking and cleaning. Even if things weren't going that well, you stayed in the marriage and made it work, at least until the kids got older.

Nothing was supposed to alter that formula.

While I tried the traditional road with all my might, in the end I just couldn't make it work. I eventually took a very different and unusual path, part of a life-long journey to find happiness. It took me a long time to get there, only after I finally accepted that life wasn't going to be the way I had planned it.

Thankfully, times are changing rapidly for fathers raising their children today.

But it's still not easy. We all struggle in our own way with our own issues, and many of the thoughts and feelings that I experienced are still the same today, despite the different circumstances. While times have changed, many of our emotions have not.

I'm telling my story now so that people can not only recognize what it was once like, but can compare it to what they might be personally going through now. By sharing my feelings maybe it will help others deal with their own. Perhaps my story can help others face their fears and conquer their obstacles in this very unique time of change.

I hope to inspire others to live life on their terms.

This is my story, from my vantage point. It is my journey.

I am sure others would have different versions of the same events, to which they are certainly entitled. This is how I experienced my life, and how I choose to tell it. These are my memories and my emotions. No one should get upset about it, because it's my take on my experiences. I'm allowed.

Ultimately I hope my story motivates other men to be great dads too, and for everyone to accept that any man can be a primary caregiver…just as much as any woman.

Let's learn from each other and face our struggles more confidently, together. By sharing stories of parenting from all walks of life, we can help future generations raise their children.

It's time to share. This is my journey, this is my story: *Out and About Dad*.

MY JOURNEY

CHAPTER 1
Living the Life?

I've always been a man with a plan, with a very clear picture of what my life would be like.

I could literally visualize it in my mind when I was younger, including what I was wearing, what my wife looked like, how we would cook in the kitchen together, and how I would rush off to work in the morning with a cup of coffee in my hand after kissing the (two) kids goodbye. I had it all laid out in my mind.

Well I don't really like coffee, but you get the point.

I've told this story many times before, at marketing industry speaking events, in business books and blog posts I've written, and with friends: I knew from a very early age that I wanted to go into marketing. I have no idea how or why, but that was my plan.

I was just one of those kids who paid attention to advertising, packaging, and brand promotions starting at a really young age. I would watch the television commercials more than the shows, read the print ads in magazines rather than the articles, scour the packaging of the brands in our house, and marvel at the in-store displays.

Yes, I studied the backs of the cereal boxes with great delight. How cool that I actually got to create them later on in my life!

As a kid I would go to the grocery store with my mother just to read the labels. When UPC codes first appeared on the scene, I was mesmerized at the checkout counter.

I was a marketing geek from day one.

I was just absolutely fascinated by how it all got done; clearly there was a lot of thought put into this brand activity and I wanted to know more about it. I wanted to learn how to do it.

As a teenager, I started asking anyone I could find to help me figure out how to be a marketer. People told me that I had better get into a good school… priority numero uno. I was on it.

To get into a good school, I figured I better show a lot of activity, business related, in high school. So I got a job at the local JCPenney, in the catalog department. I worked there all through high school and into college, taking orders over the phone and at the counter. I eventually "graduated" upstairs to the men's department where I became a champion sweater-folder. I also did some minor modeling, mostly live runway shows at the local mall where the store was located.

It was upstate New York, so trust me I was only modeling sweaters!

It is JCPenney that helped me save money for college, and gave me a love for business activity.

I remember at the time the store was trying to go upscale a bit, with a new line of Italian clothing that was much more expensive. The clothing was beautiful, but all of us in the store knew it was a tough sale, coming from what was known as a more affordable retailer. On the very first day, I sold a gorgeous navy blue cashmere sweater for $200! $200 back then was a lot of money, especially at JCPenney. The store manager gave me a big hug. I was hooked.

But I digress.

As I progressed through my four years of college at Cornell University (Class of 1985), some of the best years of my life, I started to understand that I needed an MBA if I wanted to go into brand marketing. Goal set; I was on it once again. I researched and found out that to get into a good graduate program, I first had to have solid work experience. Check.

So I participated in the on-campus recruiting program at Cornell with determination. I was driven to make it happen. I was in the career center several times a week, perfecting my resume and signing up for interviews. I was there so much that I started dating one of the work/study girls that worked there.

Let's just say I became "a regular," and so did she.

As I approached graduation, I had three job offers. I set my sights on Boston and the Carnation Company, where I joined their Management Training Program. It was a great first job but I knew it would just be a stop along the way.

I got promoted from the program pretty quickly and moved to the New York district, which was just fine because I had applied and gotten accepted into two MBA programs in Manhattan: Columbia University and New York University (NYU). I chose Columbia because I could do a dual major in Marketing and Finance, keeping my career options open. I had researched along the way that brand managers have profit and loss (P&L) financial responsibility in addition to marketing so I obviously needed that education too.

While I imagined the MBA program would be like going back to college for two more years, I immediately realized that it was more like work, a lot of very competitive work.

The place was cutthroat, I have to say, with people eyeing each other for who was going to be more successful. It didn't bother me, nor did I participate in it; I had a plan and I knew what I was doing. What others were doing didn't make a difference to me. I was in competition with myself and had my own goals. No one else mattered in the race.

I just always felt that there were plenty of jobs to go around, so everyone could win in their own way. I still feel that way.

The entire two years at Columbia were all about getting a job, and that's it. I interviewed like a pro and quickly had multiple offers for a summer internship between the two years of the MBA program.

I chose Johnson & Johnson for the summer of 1988, where I later returned after graduation the next year to begin my marketing career. Ronald Reagan may have been President of the United States, but my hero was the President of Johnson & Johnson who quickly became one of my role models.

Now at the time I remember getting a lot of grief from people who weren't quite as successful in the job market. They commented often about me having it so easy. Easy! I'd planned my whole life for this! No such thing as an overnight success. Or as my father says, "It takes a lot of hard work to be lucky."

After graduation, I was twenty-five years old and full-time at Johnson & Johnson as a marketer. I had arrived at my destination, years in the making, and it was glorious.

Please realize that I never envisioned doing this alone. A wife and kids were always in the plan. In fact, I fancied having an equally successful wife and that we would share career success while raising a family together. We would be completely equal partners, both doing our thing at home and at work. "She" was a big part of my plan.

I tell you all this to give you a glimpse into my psyche.

I'm a planner. I decide what I want and I put my head down and go for it. I knew I wanted to go into marketing for a big-time brand, so I set my sights and got it. Was it a long road and a lot of hard work? Sure was, but I knew where I wanted to go and I knew I was going to get there. None of it came easy, thank you very much, but I took each bump along the way in stride.

Were there disappointments? Sure there were, but I kept going. My mother was battling cancer most of the time I was in college. My first roommate in Boston died while he was on vacation before he ever moved into our apartment, leaving me alone in the big city.

I put my head down and I plowed ahead.

While I was satisfied with my decision to get my MBA at Columbia University, I originally, fanatically, wanted to get into the Harvard MBA program. I got quickly rejected.

Kaboom.

I was devastated. On the day I got the "ding letter," my sister saw my sadness and gave me her Christmas present weeks early…a very cool Daniel Mink watch that she'd admired for me. We both loved watches and she knew there's nothing like a little "something" to get you through life's disappointments.

I still keep that watch in a case to this day, and while it's no longer in style, it has become a symbol of "moving on" for me.

Because I always wanted a family of my own, the personal side of my life was also a big part of the plan. Get married, buy a house, have kids (a boy and a girl)…that was my destination right alongside my career. Actually, it wasn't just a destination, it was my destiny.

So of course I rushed it along and got engaged to my college girlfriend during the first year at Columbia and then got married during winter break the following year. We bought a house shortly after I graduated. I began working full time on the Monday after my last final exam. I was on a mission and couldn't wait to get started. I literally couldn't wait because I had no money, so I didn't have much of a choice.

Within six months, at age twenty-six, I had pulled a hat trick: got married, bought a house, and started a new job. Oh, and graduated with an MBA.

Looking back, what was the big rush?

Those first few years in marketing were wonderful, and the first few years of my marriage were fine too. Nothing was perfect by any means, but I was on my path; I was accomplishing what I wanted to do.

I found work incredibly fulfilling: I was good at it, and I loved the people I was working with. While at Johnson & Johnson, I launched seven new products in five years, including what became the number-one teen skincare line, Clean & Clear. It went global quickly and until just recently was still using the same tagline that I personally wrote: Clean & Clear and Under Control.

I was loving it.

While I was working a lot trying to advance my career, I still spent plenty of time at home. In fact, I was running the home.

I did the yard work, yes, as you would imagine any good husband would do. But I also did the cleaning, the grocery shopping, and in many cases, the cooking. I did all the laundry including the ironing – my wife's and my own. I picked out and bought most of her clothes for that matter.

She was just not the domestic type, and I knew that going in. I accepted it, not knowing what I was really accepting.

Unlike my experience, she was incredibly unhappy in her work or so she said. I can count on two hands how many times she cooked dinner those first few years, yet she was constantly complaining about work. If it wasn't one thing, it was another. I didn't care at all.

I kept moving forward. I kept it all together.

My work was amazing; her work was agonizing. I felt guilty for being happy at work and I felt completely responsible for her being unhappy at her work. It wasn't my fault, but somehow I felt like it was. Unrealistic, I know. Stupid, actually.

I felt like I had to keep the boat afloat even if it meant doing it by myself. I had watched for years how my parents kept our house running, so I just did the same. I never stopped to think that perhaps my plan wasn't working. I never followed traditional gender roles, so it didn't occur to me that she should be cleaning the house, and doing the grocery shopping…or at least helping. I wasn't built that way. I just took it all on, happily.

So of course, according to plan, in 1993 we decided to have a baby. I had no idea what it would mean to take care of a baby; I was completely and utterly inexperienced. But we decided to take the plunge.

Thankfully our neighbor had a baby a few months before my daughter was born, so she used to call me over when he needed his diaper changed or when he was ready for a feeding. This was her third boy, so she had already been there. I needed the practice though and she probably needed the break!

Ironically, my first assignment at Johnson & Johnson was in the Baby Products Group, but that didn't mean I could tackle a baby of my own. I knew all the ingredients that went into the No More Tears shampoo, but didn't know how to actually use it!

C'mon over, he needs a bath!

Along came my baby girl, with much happiness and amazement. We decided that my wife would stay home to raise our kids, so she never returned to her job after maternity leave. We didn't want our kids going to daycare. Thinking back, that was a mistake; daycare would have been a good thing.

Along with baby girl came a hurricane called parenthood.

While there were certainly times of joy, there was also an avalanche of more work. My wife got crushed with the storm, and I kept moving forward, taking even more on. I took it all on.

Sure, she was home all day taking care of the baby, and that is no small feat. So to compensate, I took care of the baby and the house at night, to give her a break. Many times I'd have to stop at the grocery store on the way home too, knowing there'd be no food in the house. I'd get home to a mess. I'd clean up, cook dinner, bathe the baby, and then put her to bed. If the baby had trouble sleeping at night, I got up too.

It was like work started again from the minute I got home from work. I didn't care at first, because the baby was happy and thriving.

Then I would return to work the next morning, bleary-eyed from lack of sleep and start the twenty-four hour cycle over again. As many parents say, having a baby is a study in sleep deprivation. I was a perfect specimen.

As you can imagine, it started to wear thin after a while.

As time went on, I started to feel like a servant since I added all of this onto my already crowded to-do list. We would go out with friends and I would relate more to the other mothers than the fathers. We would talk about balancing all the work at home with the work at work, not knowing how we did it all.

I commiserated with the moms, ironically, as my wife drank beer with the dads.

I will never forget the weekend that I invited a very good friend from Johnson & Johnson over for brunch. The baby was only a couple of months old and she had never "met" her.

It was Sunday morning.

It had been a particularly rough weekend with the baby, and a particularly busy week at work, and now here I was entertaining.

No rest for the weary.

After getting the baby settled for the morning, I literally had an hour and a half to pick up the house, go grocery shopping, and cook brunch before my friend came over with her husband.

My wife was sleeping in.

I got it all done, of course, because I always do…with a little help from the deli counter as I was holding the baby in her car seat. The one thing I didn't do was shower; maybe there would be time for that later.

I did it. I did it with a smile on my face because they were *my* friends coming over to *my* house to see *my* baby. It was *my* choice and *my* job. Or at least that's how it all felt.

Was it fun? No, not at all. But I felt like it was my duty.

Now of course my friend saw through the façade.

While she didn't say a word at the time, and certainly not at the brunch table, it came out months later that she was worried about me. She was worried about me taking on too much. My family was also having a fit too, witnessing me trying to juggle it all.

She wasn't the only friend who could see the real story peeking through. Other friends and neighbors started to comment on how they didn't know how I could handle it all…some of the comments turned to *why* would I handle it all.

I brushed it all off; I was a man with a plan and this was just how it was going to have to work. This is what I wanted, after all. I wanted the big marketing job, the wife, the home, and the kids. This is what I had planned for my entire life. I was going to make my plan work, come hell or high water.

It was hell. I could barely keep my head above the high water.

Oh yes of course, with great delight, we decided to have a second child in 1995. Along came a baby boy about eighteen months after my daughter was born. Now I had a boy and a girl, just what I always wanted! How could life be any better?

In all sincerity, I wouldn't change a thing in my life if it meant not having my two kids. I would put up with anything for them. No regrets, just lessons learned.

In the meantime, I made some pretty big decisions about my career to make it all come together. I left the big corporate life and went to work for a small agency where I could work from home. I did this so that I could be home with the kids.

Truthfully I had no choice but to be home to take care of the kids. I needed a much more flexible schedule with more control over my hours, even if it meant changing my career path.

I was changing my career path so that I could change diapers!

I'm sorry to say baby boy, but the first few months with my son were brutal.

He was a screamer, all day long and all night long. In the beginning, I had to learn how to prop myself up in a corner at night so that I could hold him just the right way to keep him asleep so that I could sleep a little, too. So in essence I would sleep standing up, with the two walls as my "bed."

Then I had to "get up" and go to work. It was a physical challenge, to say the least. It was also a mental challenge, trying to find the energy to focus on work the next day…every day.

I don't know why but my son just had to have human contact to fall asleep.

I can remember rubbing his little back in the crib, until he would fall asleep. I would then slowly start to remove my hand, one finger at a time so as not to wake him up. I'd finally, painfully, one finger at a time, slowly take my hand off his back, creeping backwards towards the door, only to have him wake up screaming. I'd repeat the procedure until I successfully kept him asleep and got out of his bedroom.

One night he finally slept through the night. In fact, I woke up in the morning to daylight and was convinced something horrible had happened during the night. After that one night, he slept through the night, every night. It's almost like he'd reached a physical milestone of some sort. I was happy for the change, no matter the reason!

Meanwhile, my daughter was barely two years old and getting used to a new brother, moving out of her crib, giving up her pacifier, and trying to keep active while her brother got acclimated.

Exhausting isn't even the word.

This is what a parent does. I was making it all work, no matter the cost. It wasn't about keeping score, it was about making my life work, and taking care of those two kids that I wanted to have.

I wouldn't dare acknowledge that my plan wasn't working. I couldn't stop to think if I was happy. I didn't dare open up to the looming feeling that was starting to creep into my mind.

Even when people around us started questioning why my wife was out at night and I was home with the kids, I didn't really question what I was doing. Even when she pulled into the driveway in the morning, just in time for me to pull out to go to work, I didn't really question it. Yes my heart was racing faster than the car's engine, but I kept our life moving forward. I was a husband, a dad, and a marketer. This is what I said I wanted.

I just assumed that these were going to be the terms.

Don't get me wrong, it wasn't always bad. I was thriving in my new job. I was meeting some amazing colleagues and making some really good friends. Occasionally traveling for work was a welcome respite from the burden at home, although coming home after was twice the work. Laundry piled up as did everything else.

After a while, I did finally start to "get it." I had several people whispering that perhaps this wasn't fair and I was starting to hit a breaking point.

There were nights I would cry from exhaustion, wondering if I could keep it up.

There were nights I would stare into space because for the first time in my life I didn't know what to do! My son was about six months old, I had two babies in the house, and I never felt more alone in my life.

Was it time to "go there?"

I actually started to come clean with some friends, for the first time ever, about what was going on at home. There were a couple of guys from a New York advertising agency who were particularly helpful to me. To this day, I still appreciate their objective support during that very difficult time.

I slowly started to realize that something wasn't right. It wasn't about being "fair" as so many had prompted me to contemplate. And it wasn't about having to cook and clean. I really didn't mind doing all of that. It was about the growing feeling of resentment brewing inside.

This was not the scenario I had planned. Yes, I wanted the job and the home and the kids, but not like this. Not on these terms; not in this manner; maybe not with this woman. Probably not. But with who then?

Fuuuucccck. But what did I want?

For the first time ever, I started questioning who I was, and what I really wanted. I started really questioning if my plan was the right plan.

The man with the plan was starting to crumble.

But what did I want?

Was it time to "go there?"

Then the other shoe dropped…

CHAPTER 2

The Turning Point

All I asked was why she was out so late the night before…a reasonable question in my mind.

As she threw the high-heeled black shoe at me in response, and it hurled passed my head, I made a decision. Couples fight all the time, so perhaps this should have been no different. But, this one was different. The shoe hit a nerve, and I guess it gave *me* some nerve.

My son was not even a year old and I'd had it. It was 1995, O.J. Simpson was on trial and I felt like I was in prison. I wanted out.

I literally said to myself, "You have no idea what you just did." It was the proverbial straw that broke the camel's back.

How the hell did I let it get to this?

That one shoe changed things forever. I walked out the door and went for a ten-mile run to formulate a plan. As I turned the corner at the end of the block, my neighbor waved hello to me. On the way back, he waved to me again and gestured in shock at how long I'd been running. I must have played the song *Waterfalls* six times on that run, as in "don't go chasing waterfalls."

I needed the time to think it all through.

Granted, I'd been thinking about it already. I had slowly come to the conclusion that this wasn't going to work. I had realized that the situation that I had created wasn't sustainable. I could no longer hold it all together, not like this. I could no longer uphold what I thought I was supposed to do as a husband and a father.

Not in this situation anyway.

I finally opened up my mind to the possibility of change. I started to realize that something had to change, and I had to be the one to change it. I have a couple of friends to thank for it.

The only time I could really stop to think about it was when I was traveling for work, which wasn't that often. Otherwise I'd go running to get some time to think.

I did a lot of running those days.

As Winston Churchill famously said, "If you're going through hell, keep going." I kept running.

I was starting to figure out what wasn't right, and was coming to the conclusion I just might need a different life. It was the same line of thinking that made me realize that I might not be exactly who I thought I was all these years. I could feel that I was changing, discovering what I needed to do to be happy.

Through all the intense unhappiness, I was starting to become honest with myself.

I know it seems like it should have happened in the reverse, but it wasn't until I realized how unhappy I was that I figured out how to become happy. I began to figure out what it would take to make me happy.

The current situation wasn't working, yet I couldn't visualize myself getting married to another woman. I didn't want another woman, yet I didn't want this woman either.

But what did I want? I needed to figure that part out.

These self-realizations clearly don't happen overnight; there are always a few turning points along the way. There are points of realization that make you stop to think. All of us go through this at some point in our lives. This was my time. Others have told me of their own experiences.

While I had many "moments" at home that got me thinking, I had experienced a few outside the home too.

My two New York friends actually figured it out before I did; funny how that happens sometimes. Perhaps not consciously, but they quietly coaxed and guided me into figuring it out for myself, without ever saying a word.

One night after a long meeting in New York, they asked me if I wanted to grab a drink with them; we had done this a few times now and spending time with them was very reaffirming to me. I really enjoyed their company and talking to them. They were incredibly helpful to me.

I was pretty sure they were gay and I was pretty sure they were dating, but I didn't know definitively and I didn't really care. They hadn't labeled who they were yet, and I was fine with that. I'm not that into labels.

Totally out of the blue, they asked me if I'd mind going to a local gay bar called Splash. It's no longer around, but back then it was a gay destination for locals and tourists. I didn't know that at the time, but I soon figured it out.

Although I confidently said, "Sure," *(gulp)* I wasn't completely sure. They didn't reveal too much to me ahead of time, but I liked them enough and figured, "why not."

I had no idea what was about to hit me as we walked through the front door of this place called Splash.

I immediately heard the pulsing beat of dance music. A remix of the song *One by One* by Cher was playing, which I took as a welcoming sign. Thankfully, we immediately went to the bar by the door and ordered drinks. I needed something to do with my hands.

My head was spinning.

As I pushed a lime into a cold bottle of Corona, we walked passed the bar and turned the corner into the main room. *(gulp)*

I was completely overwhelmed by what was in front of me. I felt something I'd never imagined or felt before…complete comfort.

The feeling was totally overwhelming…not intimidating and not confronting…overwhelming.

There were no sexual "tingles" at all nor did I talk to anyone else that night. That's not what I was feeling. Quite the contrary, I just stood there in disbelief most of the time, cold Corona in hand. I don't know for sure, but I bet my friends were probably watching my reaction with smiles on their faces. They never said a word about it. They just let me take it all in.

I can't even describe it; the feeling took over my entire body, but I didn't say a word.

This was not what I thought I would see at a gay bar.

There was an incredible sea of sameness; clusters of men who were all just like…me. The guys were working professionals with their friends stopping by a local bar for a drink after work. Some were in suits, some in jeans and t-shirts, but all of them were nice, normal, friendly-looking men who just happened to be gay. Many were alone, but they seemed comfortable anyway.

I acknowledged it: they all seemed just like me.

I didn't really see any of the stereotypes I had held onto all those years. I had never seen anything like it before in my life; I had never felt anything like it before in my life. I wasn't sure what to do with all of that emotion, so I just took it all in.

I did my best to carry on a conversation with my friends through the loud music, but my eyes were darting around the bar the whole time. When it was time to leave, I walked a few blocks by myself and grabbed a slice of pizza.

Comfort food for the restless mind.

They had been talking about a new movie *Jeffrey*, about gay men living in New York City. They said it was groundbreaking so I felt compelled to go see it. A few weeks later while watching the movie, I again felt an odd, unexpected emotion: jealousy. I wanted a life like that! While it wasn't a sad movie, there were points that I cried, almost on the edge of being out of control.

This was ten years before *Brokeback Mountain* came out in 2005. There were no cultural references for me. *Jeffrey* was a first and it moved me.

But it left me asking, "What is going on with me?"

Not long after, I was home with the kids one Saturday afternoon and they were particularly full of energy. We had played every game in my repertoire and we had gone outside a few times to run around. I could not tire them out!

To get a bit of a break, I popped in a videotape of the Disney movie *The Little Mermaid*, which was one of my daughter's favorites at the time. She would sing and dance to all the songs; she knew every single word!

The strangest thing happened about a third of the way in: when the signature song *Part of Your World* came on, I was instantly glued to the screen; the song took on a whole new meaning for me.

Here is my daughter singing along to the song, her voice in perfect synch with the character, dancing around toys all over the floor, and I'm the one identifying with every single word in the lyrics.

I know this sounds crazy, but it was a turning point for me in realizing who I am. As tears started streaming down my face, I realized that I was *(gulp)* gay. I realized that I couldn't avoid it, and that I had to do something about it if I wanted to move on and live a happy life.

I wanted to be part of that world.

> *Up where they walk up where they run*
> *Up where they play all day in the sun*
> *Wanderin' free wish I could be*
> *Part of that world*

I wanted to be part of that world.

How ironic that it took a Disney movie to get me out of my own set of expectations.

So you can imagine why a few weeks later when that shoe flew by my head, I made a decision. I made a decision to get out, and I realized that being gay was my way out.

I am gay, and I want out!

G-A-Y.

I kept saying it in my head, over and over, as if to get used to the idea. Of course I had to get used to the idea, it was a concept that I hadn't thought about ever before. It had *never* crossed my mind. It was a concept that I had no idea would ever apply to me. I didn't even know what it was.

G-A-Y.

I'm gay. I am gay. Hi, I'm gay. Did I tell you that I'm gay? Hello, my name's Jim, did you know that I'm gay?

I eventually graduated to saying it in front of the mirror. I kept saying it out loud, looking at myself over and over until I could say it without crying.

I've since heard other people describe their own realization as a "secret" that they first had to tell themselves before they could tell anyone else. Well let me tell you, this was a closely held secret that I had *never* told myself until that song came up in the movie.

But how could I be *sure*? This was a big move with no turning back.

I had to first test the waters, so to speak. I had to make sure. So one night when I was staying in New York, I stopped by Splash again and I put myself out there.

I made myself available, made myself open for other guys to come talk to me at the bar. In a way, I put an invisible "welcome" sign on my forehead.

It was terrifying. As I write this, I am literally putting my head in my hands as I relive the emotion – absolutely *terrifying*.

This was long before cell phones that you could play with to look busy and long before online dating when you could pre-arrange a hookup. You simply had to go to a bar and stand there alone, and either bravely go up to another guy also standing alone or wait for him to come up to you.

The thought of walking up to someone was out of the question. I would wait until someone came up to me. *If* someone ever came up to me.

As I was standing there I noticed a colleague from work on the other side of the room.

Holy shit!

I couldn't dwell on the fact that I didn't know he was gay for too long because I had to get out of sight. I quickly dashed downstairs to the lower level to avoid being seen. My heart was racing, in more than one way.

Downstairs, after going through two more bottles of beer, a cute guy did eventually come up and talk to me, and he was a sweetheart. I didn't know quite what to do, so I just tried to relax and enjoy the conversation. The music was really loud, and we were straining to hear each other. He kept getting closer and closer to me so that he could hear me better. After a while, I stopped hearing the music because I was trying to identify the cologne he was wearing, because it was taking over my senses. After talking for a while, he suggested we go sit farther in the back where it was quieter and we could talk a little more privately, or at least that was his excuse.

He kissed me.

OMG, he kissed me. That was all, just a kiss (a couple of them), but OMG he kissed me…to the pulsating beat of club music in the background. *(gulp)*

The next day I was back at work at 7:30am, working on concepts for a new skin care product. All I could think about all day was, *I kissed a boy last night*. But I knocked out twelve concept boards for the upcoming product launch regardless.

I kissed a boy last night.

I had to kiss a boy last night to see how it would feel. It felt liberating, that's the best way I can describe it. Liberating.

I'm free. I guess I really am gay.

I got used to it. I got comfortable with being gay. I realized that it did in fact apply, and I started to own it.

But I had to get out…out of my marriage and out of the life that I realized was not for me. I had to get out of being so wildly unhappy.

That's okay, I would make a plan. I was gay and I could reorient my life.

She couldn't fight me on that one. It would be entirely my fault, an easy reason to change everything without having to go through the mess of fighting over anything. It was an easy way to get out, while still being honest and telling the truth. It was a way out without fighting on the way out.

Now I had no plans to "run off to be gay." I wasn't walking away from being a dad, and I wasn't walking away from my career. I wasn't walking anywhere.

As I thought it through more, being "gay" wouldn't really change me or what I was really all about; I felt very confident about that. But it would change my life, and that desperately had to happen. I couldn't carry on any longer.

But I would still be me. I would still be "Dad." I just wanted to be out in all senses of the word.

I had the confidence to know that I was still going to be taking care of my two kids, but more on my terms, more happily. Where the confidence came from, I'm not sure. Maybe it came from *finally* understanding my situation and *fully* embracing it.

My business had grown a lot at the agency where I was working, and I had already moved into a bigger office space nearby so I didn't have to change anything at work. In fact, no one at work needed to know. I just had to change my home life; that was where I would focus my energy.

I developed an exit plan; one that included telling my wife that this all wasn't going to work and that I was gay. *(gulp)*

Did I worry about the kids? Of course. Any dad would. Did I worry that the kids would suffer because their dad was gay? Yes, I worried a lot about what others would say and do, especially as the kids got older.

The anxiety almost became a brick wall, and almost prevented me from moving forward. But deep down I knew that I couldn't let fear stop me. Somehow I knew what I had to do.

You have to understand that back then there were no role models; I didn't even really know what I didn't know. I certainly didn't know what to expect. I guess in a way I was lucky to be naïve about it all.

After having thought it through as much as I possibly could, I took the jump. At some point, you have to take the jump.

Did I worry that she would trash me? Not as much because I had a feeling that this was her ticket out as well. She was miserably unhappy, but in a different manner than I was.

She needed me to take care of the kids, no doubt about that, and we weren't exactly getting along to say the least. It was time for things to change, and if this was the stimulus we needed to do it, then I was willing to put it out there. I had a feeling she'd go along with it. If she trashed me in the process, it would be worth it. She could make it completely not her fault; I was fine with that if it got me through it.

Worries aside, I made a decision and I was going for it, no matter how tough and no matter what I had to deal with. I was alone, but I felt better now that I had a plan.

I knew a lawyer in town who had helped us buy the house, and he was my only avenue to getting some legal help. So I called him and told him the situation. He was the first person that now knew the entire story; I left out no details.

I was nervous to tell him because he seemed to be an older, very conservative, stern man. I was sincerely afraid about what he would say when I told him my story.

He was amazing. He sat there and listened, and finally said, "You've been through a lot. I'm sorry to hear that."

He put me right at ease, something I hadn't expected he'd be able to do. I came into the meeting expecting to panic right at the start.

He basically said to get a really good, gay-friendly, family lawyer…ideally a woman, and ideally a straight woman.

He said I was "lucky" that Bucks County was such a liberal county and that Pennsylvania was a no-fault state. He said that she couldn't really, in theory, do much to harm me.

Lucky?

But he also gave me a dose of reality: judges are on the mother's side, pretty much all the time. He said that I would probably be all right, but that I had to play it very safe. If she wanted to, she could make it very ugly.

Ugly?

I suddenly felt nauseous. I started to question if I could face the reality of it all.

He said that when push comes to shove, there's never enough money to go around, and that's usually when the shit hits the fan. He said that she would likely be fine until she realized that there wouldn't be enough money.

Money?

He left me with two priorities… "Get the money part straight right from the start, and let her save face."

I started to feel ugly at the thought of it getting ugly and the focus on money made me feel even more inadequate. Inevitable, I suppose. I just wanted to go home and curl up in bed, but I couldn't because I had two little kids waiting for their dad.

I walked out of his office with a slip of paper in my hand: the name and phone number of a female lawyer in Philadelphia who specialized in LGBT family matters. She was the number-one LGBT lawyer in the state. She wasn't gay, but she worked to protect the rights of gay people, and had done a lot of work with gay parents. I took a little bit of confidence knowing that.

Who knew people with this kind of expertise even existed!

L-G-B-T? Is that what I am now? Suddenly, out of nowhere, I have a label.

When I got into my car, my head was reeling. LGBT? What the hell is that? Gay rights? Is that what I need now? I'm now a gay father, and I need to have my rights protected?

I guess so.

Baby steps.

The next day I found myself, at 3:00 in the afternoon, in a downtown Philadelphia skyscraper looking at a stupendous view from a giant conference room. I knew that I was doing something huge.

I felt like I was doing something bigger than me. It was life changing and life threatening at the exact same time.

Baby steps.

When my new lawyer walked into the conference room, I couldn't help but notice that the scale was all off.

The conference room could have easily held fifty people. The view spanned what I sure was at least twenty miles in all directions. I had lost so much weight at this point that my dark grey suit was just hanging off of me, and my suit pants were bundled around my waist by a big belt so that they wouldn't fall off. In walks this woman, who couldn't have weighed more than ninety-five pounds soaking wet, dressed to the nines.

She shook my hand, all business, and gestured that I could sit down in one of the empty leather chairs that were perfectly assembled around the gargantuan table.

"Tell me what's going on," she instructed. No time for small talk.

I spent twenty minutes with her, but left feeling empowered. She made me realize that I'd be fine in the end, and she assured me that she would do everything she could to help me. And in the end, she certainly did.

She too instructed me to get the finances in order, and to make it easy for my wife to be agreeable. "Take money out of the equation," was her guidance to me, just like the first lawyer I spoke with.

I asked her how to do that, and she walked me through it step by step. I had so much more information now and felt a little better with it – even though it was all scribbled on a piece of paper I had nervously crumpled up while talking to her.

She also said I should try to get joint legal and physical custody. It wouldn't come automatically, because that's generally reserved for the mother. But she said that given the fact that I'm gay, it would be important for me to have joint legal and physical custody so that my soon-to-be ex-wife wouldn't be able to change her mind and start making decisions without me. It wouldn't necessarily be easy, but it was important.

"One more thing," she said. "Add an anti-disparagement clause if you can." Right! Never imagined in my life that I would need that!

I knew what I had to do.

The lawyer must have thought I was a mess, but she never let on to it. I met with her several times over the following months, and through the years. She eventually left the firm and the state, but referred me to another lawyer who was equally as committed and informed. The law firm took very good care of me through the years, and gave me sound advice. It's no wonder they were the best in the state for LGBT people.

LGBT.

Now all I had to do was tell my wife that she was soon to be my ex-wife and that I am gay. *(gulp)*

Baby steps.

One Saturday morning when the house was oddly and particularly quiet, I called her into the family room and said that I had something to tell her. I didn't blurt it out, but sort of coaxed my way into the announcement. Actually, I think I coaxed her into the announcement.

I have to say she handled it very well.

Part of me thinks she was expecting it and part of me thinks she was relieved. With this news flash, none of it was her fault and there was nothing she could do about it. Just like I had planned.

Did I cry? Absolutely.

Did we hug it out? Absolutely.

Was I relieved? Absolutely. I cried and I hugged from sheer (desperate) relief.

Am I glad I did it this way? Absolutely.

Did I take money out of the equation? I know how to follow good advice.

Later we scheduled when it would make sense for me to move out and I secured an apartment right nearby. We ran through the furniture in the house that I would take, and we settled out how the finances would work, at least in the short term. I made sure she was getting much more than any court would require so that there would be no reason for her to question it or to take me to court.

Take money out of the equation. It worked.

Did I get joint legal and physical custody? You betcha!

It was all completely amicable, unlike the prior months. I felt a calm I hadn't felt in months, correction, years.

For me, the hard part was over; I had a plan and I was executing it. As I had been informed, Pennsylvania was indeed a no-fault state so the minute you move out you are legally separated and on the path to divorce. The rest is just paperwork, so it makes no difference how long it takes. The stage was set; I was done.

Before I moved out, I did have my first major gay experience. I was in New York traveling on business again so I stopped by the only place I knew to go: Splash. While it was the third time I'd been there, it ended up becoming a first for me.

People would ask me for years if I had cheated on my wife and if I had any gay experiences when I was younger. Nope. This was the first. Granted, it probably should have come a lot sooner, but so be it. I was ready for my first.

By now I wasn't the least bit nervous. If anything, I was more assertive than I imagined I would be…all that pent up emotion allowed me to drop any shred of shyness. Not only did I like the feeling, I reveled in it. I felt comfortable in my body, and I oddly felt very comfortable being with a man, given the fact that I had absolutely no experience. I couldn't help but feel like I'd been missing something my whole life.

There was no pressure to perform or to do anything, and that was probably the best part. That was a first too.

Now hold on…it wasn't anything like what anyone could be imagining reading this right now. It wasn't that big, and it wasn't that dramatic, but it was breakthrough for me. All I could think about after was, *When can I do that again?*

It was time to move out and move on with a brand *new* life.

Although truthfully I was entering uncharted territory…*(gulp)*

CHAPTER 3

#SGD

The first night in my new apartment was just glorious.

I was out and it was about *me* for once.

One of the neighbors down the street helped me load my furniture into his pickup truck to move me the whopping quarter-of-a-mile to my new apartment.

It took all of about thirty minutes since I had very few things: the bed and mattress that my sister had given me from her first apartment, a sectional that my parents had given me when they moved to Virginia, an extra television we had purchased along the way, and a couple other pieces of furniture...enough to cobble together a new "home."

It was just a small, one-bedroom "flat" right in town within walking distance of the house so that going back and forth with the kids would be easy. I had every intention of being with them every day, either in my new apartment or back at my old house.

The one distinguishing feature of the apartment was a tub you stepped up to get into which on the one hand was odd yet on the other hand, surprisingly convenient for bathing the kids. I took solace in these little features because there wasn't much else to rave about.

After we moved the furniture in, I ran to JCPenney to buy a few essentials, including a plastic shower curtain with a world map on it. I also bought a glass-top dining room table from Pier One with four matching chairs. I daydreamed in the shower that night as I looked at the world, thinking through what the hell I had just done. I counted all the countries I had never heard of before, realizing how naïve I was about what makes the world go round. I never had time to daydream before.

As I crawled into bed at 9:00pm, exhausted from moving that day, I called the guy I had met in New York. We talked for an hour, but I didn't mention anything about the apartment. He knew nothing about what was going on in my life, and I wanted it that way. He just thought I was some big advertising executive who had just launched a new campaign for Aveeno skin care. He was fascinated by my work because it was so different from his, and that was all he needed to know about me at the moment.

I wanted to move on, not talk about the day's events or any of my drama. I hadn't told him about the kids yet; that would come later, maybe, if there was even going to be a "later." I was just enjoying my time with him on the phone, in my new home, and that was plenty for me.

I felt like a kid again.

I had a feeling of contentment that I hadn't felt in a very long time, probably since I was in college, actually. I just wanted to revel in it. I can remember times with my friends back then when I felt this incredible serenity – blissful happiness – a time when we were all in synch, doing well in school, and having the time of our lives. That blissful feeling came back that night. When we hung up, I drifted right to sleep and in fact slept in late the next morning for the first time in years.

Despite the back and forth with the kids, the workweek seemed suddenly so much easier.

Later in the week, the guy from New York left a message on my answering machine, and then played the song *Someone Like You* by Linda Eder.

Wow, someone actually did something nice for me! We had spoken about our mutual love for music and I guess he thought the lyrics would resonate with me. It was a nice little fling, but we never got close enough for him to meet the kids.

Even now when I drive by that same apartment, I remember that first night – it felt that good. For years when I would drive by with my daughter, she would also point out the apartment because even from her perspective it held fond memories. Thankfully.

I was only there for a year, and in that time we all slept in the one bedroom, so she remembers being able to crawl right into my bed from her bed, even though the rule was she couldn't get up until daylight. Dad had some ground rules in this home too.

My parents came a few weekends later to help me "settle in." They did the best they could: they bought me a set of very expensive blue glasses from Villeroy & Boch (which we still have) and a set of dishes from JCPenney (which are long gone). What else could they do, really? All I remember from their visit was that all of us were sitting at that glass-top dining room table from Pier One staring at the small cutout kitchen.

I think they were afraid for what could possibly come next. I found it very hard to talk to them about what might or might not happen.

"Are you able to cook for them here?" my mother asked, almost out of desperation for something to say.

"Yup."

While it was probably the worst place I'd ever lived aside from my college years, the time I lived there was probably the best year I had lived in so many ways. Sure the carpet was worn out, the kitchen was completely outdated, and the rooms were tiny, but it was still mine. I took great glory in that fact.

I was able to make my own decisions, once again.

But that didn't mean that I was ready to go public quite yet.

At first, I didn't want to tell anyone anything. I needed some time. Luckily, my ex-wife agreed to keep quiet too, and she did the best she could for as long as she could. I never blamed her for saying anything; she needed to have a reason for me moving out and it was easy to just blame me.

"Jim's gay, what can I say?" became her gateway to freedom.

My gateway was that apartment.

After it all sunk in, I was fine using that as the reason. In an odd way, I was more ashamed for getting divorced than I was of being gay. Divorce meant failure, being gay was just who I was. In an odd way, it allowed both of us to save face, just like that first lawyer told me. Plus it was true, I was gay.

Using "gay" to explain the divorce became an easy out, even for me. It allowed me to leave out a lot of the details, details that were far more painful to talk about. Information that was really no one's business.

The first person I finally told was my friend from J&J, the one who had come over to the house for brunch to meet my newborn daughter.

When I came out to her, we were standing at a crowded bar at a micro-brew pub in Princeton, NJ. I knew she was safe to tell; she'd always been so generous with her emotions and attitudes as a friend. I knew in my heart she would not only be supportive of me, but she'd be happy for me. She was just that kind of person.

I had already told her about getting divorced; she was one of the first to figure out what was going on. She was very intuitive. Her immediate reaction from that part of the story was, "I'm so proud of you." I needed that.

Then it was time to tell her the rest.

The bar where we met that night was so noisy that I had to either scream it out loud, enough for her husband and everyone else to hear, or I had to gently whisper it as if it was a closely guarded secret. I chose the latter.

As I whispered in her ear, her face lit up and she said, "I'm so proud of you." Those were her first words. I needed that.

After I told her my "news," she whispered in her husband's ear and he threw in a thumbs-up. I know it sounds cheesy, but it was the best thumbs-up of my life; I can still picture the scene today, including the blue denim shirt he was wearing.

I was wearing an ill-fitting, faded maroon Gap sweater and a worn-out pair of Levis, both of which just hung off of me. I weighed 158 pounds…I hadn't been eating much lately and I was running at least five miles a day. Often longer. I walked out of that bar on cloud nine, arm in arm with my friend. I needed that.

While she was the first I told, the avalanche was not far away.

There was a small town about ten miles up the Delaware River called New Hope. Remarkably, it was one of a few very gay communities in the country at the time: Provincetown, Ogunquit, San Francisco, and New Hope. How odd that it was only a few miles away from me. Fate?

New Hope was a gay destination with a couple of gay clubs that filled up on the weekends. The place to go dancing was the Cartwheel, and it soon became the place where I would go to meet other gay men. There was always a friendly crowd at the Cartwheel and it wasn't that hard to meet people there.

I'd go out on the dance floor and pretty soon I'd be talking to someone. It was at the Cartwheel that I conquered the fear of dancing by myself.

Oh dancing with myself oh oh oh oh

I should clarify that: it wasn't hard to get a date at the Cartwheel. It was very hard, much harder than I would have thought, to meet friends because every guy I met just wanted to date, not necessarily be a friend.

I quickly had to get used to that because I was not prepared for it mentally.

It took me a while to master this phenomenon...and it was by far the hardest part about meeting other gay men...deciding if the guy you were meeting would become a date or become a friend. I'd never had to think about things that way before. I was searching for friends at this point more than anything else. Friends were the priority for me, but I'm not sure that was the case with most of the guys I was meeting.

But hey, I'd take a date if that was the only option! I needed that.

I was quickly schooled that Monday night was locals' night in New Hope, so I made every possible attempt to be there so that I could meet locals, even if it meant paying for a babysitter that I couldn't afford. I was more likely to make friends on locals' night than a crowded Saturday night, or at least that was my hope.

I did a lot of hoping in New Hope.

As I was still getting used to the whole situation, I was caught in a very unusual spot. On the one hand I wasn't really ready to let the straight world know that I was divorced, and newly gay, yet I wasn't ready to let the gay world know that I had just recently come out and had kids.

Talk about being stuck between a rock and a hard place!

It turned out to be something I couldn't control, as something unexpected happened to blow it all up on me.

There was a men's shop in New Hope where I went quite a bit, mostly because there was nothing else like it in the area. I loved clothes and I loved to shop so of course I went there a lot. They had the best shirts.

Because I was in the store so often, I became talkative with the owner and he would hang out with me while I tried on shirts, jeans, or whatever new items had come in. Every time I would go in he would show me what was new and convince me to try it on. Not sure how or why, but one day he took my phone number off of a credit card transaction and called me at home when I had the kids with me.

This is long before caller id, so I blindly answered the phone.

"Hello?"

He caught me off guard and he could hear the kids in the background, so I confided in him.

As fate would have it, he turned out to be a good friend of one of my old neighbors; she didn't know my story yet. He spilled the beans to her who spilled the beans to the other neighbors, and then the whole town spilled the beans. I learned a hard lesson on a rare occasion when I actually opened up… he told two friends, then she told two friends, and then she told two friends. I guess it was inevitable anyway. The cat was out of the bag.

I was out. And my ex-wife was out of having to take any responsibility. So be it.

Divorced, kids, gay. Hello?

I was called a coward during this time, if you can believe that.

"Coward?" Hardly.

Walk in my shoes, and then tell me I'm afraid to confront my issues. I was dealing with my issues every minute of every day, thank you very much!

Imagine living constantly on the edge of your seat, waiting for people to probe just a little deeper on your marriage, or about your kids, or about what you did over the weekend. Imagine having to tell a schoolteacher that your kids have a gay father and you're worried about the other kids finding out and that you're worried that your kids will be bullied. Imagine having to tell a guy you have a major crush on that you have kids, only to see him put his hands up in the air and walk away shaking his head.

Go ahead and call me a "coward."

As I had hoped, not much with the kids changed, even though my entire life was turning on its head. I was still the primary caregiver at night after work. Changing their diapers, feeding them dinner, and giving them baths…that was my nightly routine. I was still the one taking them to doctor appointments and doing all the things I had always been doing. Oh yes, I was still up to my eyeballs in dirty diapers and laundry; I was still Dad.

I would always be Dad, I never doubted that. I would never let anyone take that away from me.

My ex-wife kept our house, which was my idea, and not a lot changed there from my vantage point either. Like me, she started dating a lot, which I'm sure was good for her too. She needed to move on as much as I did.

I met most of the guys she dated, and they were all very nice to me. Some of them I knew already from around town, which was neither comforting nor awkward. I didn't let it be. They were obviously told what was up with me, but never seemed to hold it against me.

Actually, looking back, we both dated like we'd never dated before: the butcher, the baker, and the candlestick maker. Literally.

Who could blame either one of us?

She was home with the kids during the day because we had agreed that she would do that until both kids were in school fulltime, which was still a few years away. I took the kids at night, most nights, unless I was traveling for work, which she was always cool about.

We got along quite well, I have to say, for two divorced parents. We never showed the kids that anything was wrong, at least not that I remember or remember hearing about.

The whole situation was just much better and I hoped that it would stay that way. I had to make sure that it stayed that way. I had put all the crap behind me and held no anger, none at all.

Her "mom" friends still treated me very kindly, which was a good thing considering that I saw them all the time at the kids' activities.

But I couldn't get too comfortable because I never knew when the other shoe would drop. What if the situation changed and she turned on me? What if she met someone who didn't approve or accept me? It could have easily happened. It's happened to others.

For the first time in my life I had to really worry about "approval," "acceptance," and "what-if." For the first time in my life I was a minority and had minority status.

How could that be? I didn't anticipate that in my plan.

Single gay dads weren't exactly embraced, approved, or accepted. There weren't very many of us to be accepted, at least not visibly.

But I have to say that juggling work and family was actually a lot easier now, because at least there was some sort of separation to help me manage it all. It was a welcome relief to just concentrate on me, the kids, and work... nothing else.

It was my world now, on my terms. I was "part of that world," finally.

The dating part of that world came pretty naturally, to tell you the truth. Dating a man wasn't really any different than dating a woman, except that it felt a whole lot more comfortable, *finally*.

I very quickly discovered that people are people, regardless of the gender. Meeting men and going on dates and going through the "courting" was really no different than doing it with a woman. People are people, and dating is dating. I just liked dating men better.

It struck me funny how easily I fell into the rhythm of dating men...proof that I really was gay all along. It was actually so much easier than it ever was with a woman. Being with a guy never gave me pause, not once.

Wish I had known that a lot sooner.

The tricky part was that I had to manage dating like it was a job, so that I could make sure that the kids were either with their mom or with a baby-sitter who could drive at night.

Do you know what it costs to hire a babysitter that can drive at night? I was rolling quarters to pay for a night out, so spending an hourly rate on an adult babysitter was a luxury.

It kept my options limited in terms of making plans, making it almost impossible to join the "community." I found a couple of older babysitters who were in graduate school, and they saved my life. My dating life, anyway.

I longed to join a group of friends that I could hang out with, but being a working dad made that virtually impossible.

Most of the guys I met, if they were interested, were free of any responsibility yet I wasn't available most of the time. I generally kept the kids out of the conversation until I really knew the guy well, which made it very hard to get to know anyone.

How could they really know me if they didn't know that I had kids?

Ugh.

And if I'm telling the truth, I was still trying to keep a façade alive. I hadn't really told many people about the divorce, in fact no one at work knew. I hadn't told any of my college friends either. That came later in the form of personal notes I wrote to each of my fraternity brothers.

I'm not sure what I was waiting for; I guess I was just gearing up for the scrutiny that I knew would come along with my news.

So there I was, living alone in an apartment, juggling kids back and forth, dating men for the first time in my life, keeping an aggressive schedule at work, but not letting anyone really into my story.

Ugh.

While I felt more alive than I had in years, it was wearing on me.

Work consumed the entire day, the kids consumed the entire night, and both of those things consumed the entire weekend...with some dating along the way.

Then my parents announced that they wanted to take the entire family to Disney World, including my sister and my ex-wife. Wow...talk about keeping up a façade! It almost killed me, but I did it for the kids and my parents. I was trying to keep everyone engaged and intact. It was too much.

You could see the stress on my face; I had the worst acne breakouts of my entire life, even more than in high school. I started getting intense headaches every afternoon around 3:00, like clockwork.

I felt perpetually tired, so much so that the doctor said I was on the way to Chronic Fatigue Syndrome if I didn't deal with it. At one point my mouth broke out in a series of sores that covered the entire inside of both cheeks.

The doctor said it was stress. I called it agony.

But how could I slow down? That's impossible when you're a working, single dad...let alone a single gay dad trying to make a new life with two kids in tow.

Single gay dad: SGD.

I literally had no one to turn to. I didn't know anyone else like me; no one I knew was dealing with all of these issues all at once. I'd hear moms talk about juggling it all and I could relate to them on some level, but none of them were gay men trying to live in a new world. The men I was meeting didn't have kids, and many of them didn't want kids, so there was no support there.

SGD: the only one of its kind, at least that I knew.

I think that was the crux of the stress I was under: I was trying to live in three different worlds:

> *Dad: a single one.*
> *Working professional: an ambitious one.*
> *Gay man: a brand new one.*

SGD. If it were today, there would be a hashtag for it. #SGD.

No wonder I had the world's biggest zit on my face, hadn't had my haircut in weeks, wasn't sleeping properly, and looked like the cat just dragged me in.

Not a good look for making new friends or catching dates.

But despite all of that, I was happy, really happy, and I was in control of my life. I was a SGD and it was okay that I was alone; I had gotten used to that. It felt better than where I had been, that's for sure. While this was way before "It Gets Better," I knew in my heart that this was temporary and that things would get better. It had to get better; there was no way to go but up.

But in order for that to happen, I had to learn to face some scrutiny…

CHAPTER 4

The Most FAQ

To this day, people are unbelievably curious about how it all happened... how on earth did I ever get married and have kids, and then get divorced and come out?

How did I not know I was gay?

It's by far the most frequently asked question I get, no matter where I go and who I talk to, and no matter how many years have passed. The line of questioning starts whether I'm in a personal or a business setting; people just want to know.

I've gotten used to it, and I now see it as a sign of caring, but there was a time when it was really hard for me to take. It was really hard to handle when I first came out.

The honest answer, whether you believe it or not: "I didn't know I was gay." Sorry to say, folks, but I didn't know I was gay.

I didn't know I was gay!

I know it's hard to believe; I understand that. Most people figure it out way before I did. I had a lifetime of experiences as a "straight" man before I ever even thought I might be gay. I was in my early thirties!

I have literally, publicly and privately, been harassed on this point: how could you not have known before you got married? How could you go on to have kids and not know you are gay?

I remember a year or so after I came out, I was at a very fancy dinner party with about forty people. A gay couple I had recently met was hosting it at their farm in Bucks County, PA, about a half hour from where I lived. It was a beautiful summer night and I was so happy to be included. Not everyone was gay, but everyone was fabulous, at least upon first sight.

It was the most gay-friendly dinner party I had ever been to, I can tell you that.

The party started out with cocktails out in the wildflower garden...you could only get to it by walking along a little babbling brook lined with flowers. All the guys were wearing jeans or linen pants with casual summer shirts, dressed to perfection. The ladies were wearing light summer dresses that were just oh-so-right for the occasion. There were handsome waiters in tight t-shirts serving iced cocktails and appetizers. It was the most beautiful night I had ever experienced.

We later sat down for dinner at a long rectangular table, with about twenty or so people on each side. It was starting to get dark, and the only light came from candles running down the length of the table and from chandeliers that were strung from the tree branches above. Nestled between the candles on the table were hundreds, if not thousands, of fresh flowers that had been cut from the garden that day.

It was the most stunning table I had ever seen. I was smiling from ear to ear.

Just as we were sitting down, one gentleman (I use the term loosely) started in on me. He was the boyfriend of another guy I had met earlier; they were both very successful gay men from New York City. They had been together for years, and they could have been role models for me, or at least that's what I first hoped.

I quickly realized that would not be the case as he started his questioning. He had heard me say to someone else that I had two kids.

"You have kids," he interrupted. "How? Aren't you gay? You were married?!"

I felt like I was under a firing squad, being shot down for being a gay divorced father. It's a wonder that I didn't run back into the closet.

As this "gentleman" asked me question after question, he started getting louder and louder – I guess because he found my answers harder and harder to believe. His voice caught the attention of the entire dinner table, and a hush fell over the crowd. I had never known exactly what that expression meant, but

I learned it the hard way at that dinner table.

I'm not sure if everyone else was interested in my answers too, or if they wanted to ask their own questions, or if they were just mortified and paralyzed by what they were watching unfold.

"How could you not know you were gay?! You must have had an affair!"

As more and more questions came, I got more and more embarrassed, and I got redder and redder as sweat started pouring down my face. I wasn't prepared for this at all. It had been such a pleasant night, and suddenly the beautiful fresh flowers and glowing candles all faded from my sight. He knew he had me and didn't stop. He went in for the kill. Worst of all, he was also a gay man…an older gay man who should have been kinder.

A new friend next to me started shouting at him to stop, and kept saying to me, "Don't answer that question; you don't have to answer that question." Eventually, thankfully, people started talking amongst themselves, as a signal to move on. Eventually he must have gotten bored with my answers and turned to his partner to start a different conversation.

He shrugged me off. I was mortified, and drenched in sweat.

The couple hosting the party walked over with a fresh drink, gave me a hug in my chair, and one of them kissed me on the top of my head. While that was very sweet of them and I needed the love that very instant, I couldn't help but feel like a little kid at Thanksgiving who was sitting at the adult table where I didn't really belong.

The two hosts wound up being very supportive of me when I needed encouragement over the next year. Although they lived on a multi-million dollar estate, they would come to my modest apartment when I couldn't get a babysitter. The man who was sitting next to me at that dinner party is still among my most favorite friends, as you can imagine.

My response to that "gentleman" at the table then is still the same now: all I can say is that I didn't know I was gay.

I didn't know I was gay.

The schmuck didn't believe it. Many others don't believe it. But all I can say is that I didn't know. I never had those "feelings" and I never had a "college experiment." I never had a torrid, heated, "man-romance" that would have set me "not straight."

No such luck.

In some ways I wish I had. Looking back, I do remember wanting male companionship and wanting to make male friends, but it was never sexual. Never. I think all guys want other male friends. I see how my son hangs out with his friends; that's all I wanted when I was his age too.

I guess being gay just wasn't on my radar, as odd as that sounds.

You have to realize that growing up there was never any mention of "gay." I never saw or met or even heard of anyone being gay. It never came up. Never.

As a child growing up in Syracuse, New York, there wasn't anything that would trigger "being gay" for me. Syracuse was very isolated at the time. I had never even been to a beach until I was in college!

While my parents were conservative, they were also extremely social, having numerous parties at the house and their friends' houses. Their crowd of friends were such social butterflies and so stylish, all of them. I'm sure that's where I got my own sense of style and my fascination with colorful shirts, along with a desire to entertain in my own perfectly clean and wonderfully decorated house.

But they were all straight. I think.

Growing up we used to get all dressed up and have big formal dinner parties almost weekly, usually buffet style because there were so many people to feed. My mother was gorgeous, especially at these parties. I used to watch her get ready and put on her makeup. A lot of times she'd ask me what to wear for the night, often because I had picked it out while we were shopping.

Nope, I didn't know I was gay.

My father was a master host; no one left hungry and no one ever had an empty drink in their hand. He was much tamer in his style, but he was the type of guy that everyone loved to talk to because he was always just so calm and happy.

In addition to learning how to entertain from my parents, I also gained my adoration for all types of music, and I learned not to be shy when it comes to dancing. The bigger the beat, the better the dance moves! While I loved the beat for sure, I was also enamored with the lyrics. It was like poetry for me, much like writing for advertising eventually became poetry for me.

When we finished eating (which never came soon enough) then I would play DJ with the latest disco music of the era. It was the late '70s, after all!

As Casey Kasem, host of American Top 40, would say, "If the beat gets to the audience, and the message touches them, then you've got a hit."

My father would push all the furniture to the side in the family room and we'd have a makeshift dance floor. I had every top disco record on the charts, including every album from Donna Summer. Every song I played was a chance for me to get everyone dancing, and I got so much attention. *Hot Stuff!*

To this day, I make sure the song *MacArthur Park* is the first song played in every new place we move into. It's how I personally bless each new home, year after year, as we moved through life.

Nope, I still didn't know I was gay.

I suppose things should have changed when I moved from home and went to college, but they didn't. If I was young today, I'm sure they would have.

As a freshman, I joined a fraternity and had a blast on every level. Was it about hanging out with other men? No! It was a social extravaganza like you'd expect at a place like Cornell. I had friends around all the time, with lots of girls too. I dated girls just like all the other guys, and yes, I enjoyed it.

Because I loved to dance, I never had a problem meeting girls. I think most of them invited me to their sorority formals because they knew I would dance all night with them, non-stop.

Nope, I didn't know I was gay and neither did they.

It was social; there were no red flags.

Cornell University and the town of Ithaca, NY are very liberal, so even as we progressed into junior and senior years and the term "gay" started to be bantered around, it never occurred to me that the label would apply to me. It never occurred to me, even after one of my best friends confessed his sexual orientation to me right before graduation. There's an awkward term that was so common back in the day: sexual orientation.

It also never occurred to me years later when a close work colleague I had hired "suddenly" died from AIDS. I was sad for the loss, but I processed his death in ignorance and realized that I hadn't known he was gay. It hadn't occurred to me; I hadn't noticed. I was so naïve.

I met my now ex-wife while I was at Cornell and it was classic college dating. I was in a fraternity and she was in a sorority, so it was a hop, skip, and a jump from party to party. I was a senior and she was a sophomore. I was just a few short months away from graduation, and I just wanted to have fun.

I can only imagine what life would have been like had I let that relationship fade after college, like so many do.

I know now that I should have graduated and moved on, but I think looking back, I just so intensely wanted to get married and have kids that I hung on way too long. I was supposed to get married and have kids, according to "the plan." All of my college friends were getting hitched, and some were having kids before I even got engaged. I wanted to do the same, I really did. I always saw myself being a father; there was just no way that wasn't going to happen.

But I had to be married to a woman to have kids, obviously. There were no other options at the time.

So I stuck to my guns and despite a few bumps I pushed forward with the relationship, and advanced it to the next level after she graduated from Cornell and even after I went back to graduate school.

I guess, looking back now, I just got caught up in the momentum of it all… way too many years of momentum, and never stopped to think about it. I never questioned if it was the right thing to do or not. I never stopped to make sure it was what I really wanted.

I never stopped to really make sure that "she" was the one. I never stopped to make sure I wanted a "she."

I never stopped, that's the truth. The momentum took over.

So the decade of the 1980s became ten years of getting my plan in order. I graduated from high school in 1981, then college in 1985. I went back to graduate school in 1987, got married in 1989, and then graduated again in 1989. I went to work on my career in 1989 too.

1989 was a big year for me, and a gallon of gas cost ninety-seven cents. $0.97.

There was no *Queer Eye for the Straight Guy* to make me over, and there was no Andy Cohen from *Bravo* who I could have looked to as a role model. It's a shame, because life would have been different had there been *anything* that I could point to and say, "Hey, that's me."

So I went along the same path that every other little boy in that era did and followed in the footsteps of what you were "supposed to do." I found a girlfriend, I got married, and I had kids, in that order. There was no room for a gay fling in that equation.

I didn't know I was gay because there was no way that I could have known I was gay. It wasn't until I became insanely unhappy in my situation that I realized that perhaps, just maybe, somehow, there could be a different way to approach life.

Once I accepted the fact that my path wasn't working, I opened up my mind to other paths. Then and only then was I ready to start reading the messages to myself. And no, my ex-wife didn't "make me gay." I would never pin that on her. We were both young and in hindsight we were not ready for the life we created. I'm not sure either of us wanted it. My intense unhappiness is what ultimately opened my mind.

I don't know how else to explain it because it's the truth…I didn't know I was gay.

Shortly after I came out, so did Ellen on *Ellen* with a little help from Oprah. The timing was ironic and iconic. It gave me a burst of confidence to really start telling people, because at least now it was being talked about in pop culture, in a more positive way.

I thank Ellen for that. She faced a lot of prejudice for it at the time, and a lot of scrutiny about her life.

But sadly, like Ellen, once I did figure myself out, it could be used against me…

CHAPTER 5
Enter The Journal

The one skill I have, above anything else, is the gift of falling asleep. I can sleep anywhere: car rides when I was a kid, library chairs while studying in college, airplane seats while traveling on business, lounge chairs at the beach. I've already established the fact that I can even sleep standing up.

But like every other parent, the kids are what keep me up at night. That's true of any great parent; kids are our greatest love, but they are also our greatest worry. Even now they can keep me up at night even though they are all grown up.

For me at the time, it was always my fear of losing the kids that would make me toss and turn. The potential that they could be taken away from me because I was a gay man was my greatest fear.

Many divorced parents hold this fear, especially fathers, but mine had a gay twist. It was my fault. I decided to go public with it. I could have kept it all a secret like so many did at the time.

But what if she turns on me? What if she suddenly decides that she doesn't want me around the kids? What if she turns them against me? What if she isn't really okay with me being gay? What if she tells them that being gay is bad and immoral?

What if?

These questions were quite realistic; it was happening all around us in our culture and there would have been very little I could do about it. The year my daughter was born in 1993, Bill Clinton allowed gays to be in the military, but it came with a clear and lasting message that lasted for years: "don't ask, don't tell." Keep your mouth shut and you *might* be okay.

I used to think to myself late at night, *I just have to get them to eighteen and then we'll be safe.* If I kept my mouth shut, I *might* be okay.

Here's what I really worried about: while I was able to use the gay card to get out, she could use the gay card to get the kids away from me. It had happened to other gay people…I had met some through the years and heard all their stories. So I couldn't with 100% certainty say that it couldn't happen to me.

It was a real possibility. It wouldn't have mattered how close I was with the kids, she could take them away from me. Deep in my heart I never thought she would, but she could so I had to be realistic.

Mothers had the law on their side, hands down. They also had the court of social opinion on their side as well. But now there was a new, looming fear starting to emerge that made it even worse. As I saw my ex-wife become more and more involved with the Catholic Church, my fears really expanded. How could they not? I had to be realistic. Catholics didn't really have a great history of accepting gay people.

Sure, she was playing along with me now, but what if that changed? What if the Church changed her mind about me?

I had to be realistic.

She showed no signs that this could be the case, but I couldn't be sure she wouldn't change her mind. There are a lot of rules to follow in the Catholic Church. Granted, the Church is opening up now, finally. But not then.

I remember one time pulling out of her driveway after dropping off the kids, as one of her Church friends was stopping by. He came up to my car window and gave me a full-on lecture about putting Christ into my parenting, and how important Christ should be in my life. He and "He" promised to save me.

It was very easy to imagine how her cooperation with me could potentially turn the other way.

My best defense was to be a great father. To paraphrase Oprah, "excellence is the best defense against prejudice!"

I realized that I had to be more public about it. Aside from taking care of the kids at home, I also needed to be out with them as much as possible. I knew that I might need witnesses one day, so I had to make sure I was covered. I had to get much more open about talking about my life and how I spent my time with the kids.

While I had plenty of witnesses for when I was still married, I needed some as a SGD.

But would that be enough?

If I ever needed it, the best witness I could have was a journal I was keeping on a daily basis: a little book worth its weight in gold, and then some.

My lawyer had given me some very sound advice that I never would have thought of on my own: keep a journal of when you have the kids, all the school activities, and all the doctor appointments.

According to her and apparently according to the law, this journal could be evidence of being a primary caregiver. Nights slept in the home, school events attended, and doctor/dentist appointments completed are all proof of parenthood.

Proof?

I had to get over the fact that I might need proof.

Well, I had proof in abundance so no worries there…check, check, and triple check. Even when the kids didn't sleep with me, I still went over to the house to watch them so that their mom could do whatever she needed to do. There were nights, weeknights, where I would be over at the house until 11:30pm, waiting for her to get back. And then I was up the next morning for work, yet I needed proof.

It's funny how life sends you signals, and how support can come from surprising places.

When I was a senior in high school, I really, ever so badly, wanted to go to Cornell University for college. It was kind of like when I wanted to go to Harvard for my MBA. That never happened, but Cornell did. It's the only place I applied for college and I applied early decision.

The man with a plan had his sights set on Cornell.

No one thought I'd get in. No one. Not my teachers, not my parents – no one, except Mrs. Myers, my guidance counselor. She told me that if I wanted to go to Cornell, then damn it, I was going to Cornell, even though no one from our high school had ever gone there.

The day after I was accepted, she was the first person I told.

At graduation, she handed me a blank journal with these words handwritten:

Dear Jim,

With your superb intelligence I'm confident you will find some clever use of this book! I am very proud of your accomplishments, Jim, and more importantly of your style in relating beautifully to others. "Good luck" at Cornell and in the years to follow.

Love,
Joyce Myers ☺

Note the smiley face! "I am very proud of you."

No one had ever given me these kinds of compliments!

She signed it Joyce Myers, not Mrs. Myers. The pride and unbelievable peer-to-peer support was not lost on me. I was eighteen years old and it gave me the confidence I needed to go on to Cornell; confidence that I still draw upon to this day.

I had kept that blank journal blank for many years, carrying it from home to home as I moved through life. Now I finally had a good use for it: to protect my kids. I only wish Mrs. Myers knew, although I'm betting deep inside that she knows I put it to good use.

So while at first I started just tracking nights and days, as the months and years went on I found it necessary to get more and more descriptive about what was going on. The more notes I had, the better the proof.

This was my first entry in that very special journal:

JOURNAL: 5/11

In high school, Mrs. Myers gave me this journal and told me that one day I would find a use for it. 20 years later I finally did!

I kid you not.

I chronicled every night I had the kids, every school event, every doctor's appointment, and dentist visits too, because I could and I needed to. I wrote any relevant activity from their mom, to show that I was the primary caregiver. Let me tell you, if that journal could talk, it would make amazing binge watching on Netflix.

I certainly put that journal to good use. Thank you, Mrs. Myers. I filled it up pretty fast so I had to move on to multiple spiral notebooks.

My posts weren't long paragraphs, just quick snapshots of what I had done with the kids that day, what nights they slept with me, and what their mom was up to. Sort of like a modern-day tweet.

JOURNAL: 6/6
Today is Wed and tonight is (my son's) graduation from Kinder-
garten. He called me @ work and is all excited. I will leave work
a bit early, run home to pick up my camera, and then go to
(Mom's) house to get him dressed. I have his clothes pressed and
in my car.

Not a soul knew about that journal until now.

I was intensely consistent at first and then over time, I would stop and start, depending on what was going on in life…depending on how secure I felt as a gay father. I finally stopped writing entries when I figured the kids were old enough to have their own opinions. I knew I could always start up again, at least until they were eighteen. I still have those journals locked away for safe-keeping…no one on this earth has read them in their entirety, and no one ever will.

Here was my last entry, and although it was a long one, this snapshot captures the essence of how I was feeling at the time:

JOURNAL: 1/22
Have not felt the need to document in a while, but here we go
again. The past year or so has been business as usual. Lots of
typical stuff like rearranging weekends to accommodate her
schedule esp. for retreats.
I'm again getting concerned that (her) religious affiliation is
starting to become a controlling device. I'm worried that she's
going to turn on me and make things hard.

I decided to call the lawyer and get some advice.

Fortunately, I have not needed to write in that journal ever since, and I made it to their eighteenth birthday with both kids.

Eighteen.

Today with gay parents so mainstream in most places (though sadly not everywhere), this all probably sounds paranoid. I feel paranoid now just writing about it. But you have to remember that back then I really had nothing on my side and no one who would have defended me. Sure it was just the late 1990s and not that long ago, but times were very different when it comes to the topic of gay parenting.

Even my parents were worried.

My parents maintained a close relationship with the kids' mom all through the years, including regular phone calls, birthday gifts, and holiday visits. It pissed me off at the time, but I also understood on some level. They told me that if anything ever happened, they needed to maintain a relationship of some sort with her to be able to see the kids. It was always about the mom.

I got it – keeping close ties with the kids' mom was their "journal."

The problem was that a lot of people empathized with her, which is something I created when I came out. But now it carried great risk.

"Poor thing."

"What a shame."

"How awful."

"But how is she doing?"

It was my fault, given how I chose to frame the divorce. So there were no condolences for me, although there was a consistent acknowledgement that I was a good father. I appreciated that part at least.

Everyone worried about her, assuming that I had caused all of it. Even my friends and family would constantly ask me about her. When anyone would hear about me being gay or about any struggle with the kids, empathy was always for her instead of for me.

One of my family members even said to my face, "How typical."

Really? Not so much. At least they said it to my face; makes me wonder what they were saying behind my back. Scratch that – I'd rather not know.

As a result, I was convinced that that anyone could turn on me if she decided I needed to be gone, or if she decided to somehow "punish" me.

Again, to be fair, she never did…but the fear was always looming. I had to face it.

So I wrote in that journal every day, sometimes multiple times, just to give me some sort of a safety net and to prove "normalcy" on my side. Even though I couldn't say anything out loud, I captured my time and my thoughts in that journal.

While everything went in that journal, I said nothing out loud publicly even when I really wanted to…

CHAPTER 6

Agree to Agree

I have a fundamental principle when it comes to divorce, no matter the situation: agree to agree.

Agree to agree, no matter how hard it gets.

I don't mean to sound preachy, but I really don't understand why divorced parents fight. The two adults are done, so get over it. The kids are going through enough as it is, so why expose them to any more than they need to see? Trust me, I'm not saying it's easy, but it's essential to co-parenting of any form.

I was lucky, in a way, because my kids were very young; I'm not sure that they really knew what was going on. I'm sure I never gave them enough credit for understanding what was going on, but I wanted to minimize the impact any way that I could.

I made my own personal decision that I wasn't going to let the kids see behind the curtain; there was no reason they ever had to see any upset from me or from their mother.

I always tried to take the high road; luckily my journal helped me.

So I made a decision to "agree to agree." I was not going to argue with their mother, and certainly not in front of the kids. Ever. I promised myself that they would never see me fighting, and I would never disparage her in front of them.

JOURNAL: 2/16
(Mom's) birthday. Took everyone to dinner – had a cake at apartment with (her friend).

I think she made the same decision, because we never really got into it in front of them. Anything we needed to talk about, we took it backstage and I never heard of her disparaging me either. And she was always nothing but warm and polite publicly to anyone else in my life too. Happily, I never had to exercise the disparagement clause in our divorce.

You can never be too sure when you're a SGD. I didn't want that to ever change.

Sure, fear gave me some added incentive to get along with her, but I really do feel like I would have tried even as a straight father. It's vitally important for kids to not only have a loving parent, but to love in return. I would never do or say anything that would jeopardize that.

I am human, so I'm sure I may have slipped here or there through the years, but certainly not consciously, maliciously, or purposefully. I'm pretty sure that the kids would defend me on that one. I'm hoping she acted in a similar manner; I've never heard otherwise.

Divorced families have it hard enough, there's never a need to let the kids in on any more angst than they are already going through. Add in a gay dad, and trust me, there's plenty enough angst to go around.

I didn't need any more drama in my life than was already there, so I worked very hard to keep the peace, constantly.

I basically saw my ex-wife every single day for years, picking up and dropping off the kids. We had to go to school events together and we celebrated the kids' milestones together. We had to make decisions on the kids' lives, so in my mind we had to agree to agree. I smiled through it all.

Agree to agree.

I only expected the same in return. I certainly didn't expect any support from her; I only expected to be able to get along. But it wasn't just their mom I had to appease. I had to make a concerted effort to get along with everyone, all the time. I worried about any form of alienation from anywhere.

I made sure we all got along, and it was a constant, concerted effort.

JOURNAL: (August)
We had a birthday celebration for (my daughter). We invited
(Mom) and (her grandmother) as well. (Mom) talked about
herself, and even yelled at (my daughter) for interrupting.

It's a very odd feeling...the need to be on the defense all the time with everyone. I always had to be on my best behavior.

But I was right to some extent, and soon learned that prejudice was right around the corner...

CHAPTER 7

My First

It's a feeling I can't really describe.

One day you're in the majority, an adult white male. And then the next day you're a minority, an adult gay male and people have a problem with who you are.

It's a feeling I can't really describe.

I was prepared for it, feared it for months, and was ready for it when it hit me the first time. But it's a feeling that prevents or delays many people from coming out, me included.

The problem for me was that the prejudice didn't just start when I came out; it was there while I was married too.

I guess being an active father was a bit foreign to people at the time.

Dad wasn't supposed to be so attentive – that was mom's job. Dads were there to videotape the fun times, not to actively organize them. Certainly not shop for them or clean up after them.

Long before I got divorced, I was having dinner at Olive Garden with the kids one night, who were making a bit of a fuss at the time…making a big mess and being kind of loud. But it was Olive Garden, "When you're here you're family." I didn't make much of it, given the surroundings.

I was doing my best to keep them in control, although admittedly it wasn't a shining moment for Dad.

There was a table of women sitting next to us, who apparently didn't appreciate the "show." I don't necessarily blame them, but hey, it's the Olive Garden, not a five star restaurant by any means.

They appeared to be a group of moms, on what we would now call a "girls' night out," but I can't be sure. One of them said something to me that I didn't catch (my son was making a lot of noise), so I asked her to repeat it. Big mistake.

She repeated it much more loudly, "If their mom was with you, this wouldn't be happening. Where is the mom?"

What? "The mom?"

I decided to ignore it, because I didn't like the implication that fathers couldn't handle their kids. I guess she didn't think I could hear her, so she repeated it again, and this time the kids heard her.

The kids stopped and stared at me too, probably wondering why this woman was asking about their mom.

I stared her straight in the eyes. I leaned over so that the kids couldn't hear and loudly whispered, "She's dead." I said it just to shut her up and to embarrass all of them. They didn't say another word the rest of the night.

It was my first confrontation with prejudice, but certainly not the last.

It wasn't easy being a dad. It's not easy for anyone actively involved in their children's lives.

I'd be at school events or other activities with the kids, and I mostly stood by myself. I kept to myself most of time. Not just because I was gay but also because I was often the only father there. The mothers were in their cliques and I was alone.

Women weren't exactly on my side because they didn't have husbands like me. Husbands weren't at all on my side because they couldn't relate to me and they probably didn't like the message I was sending to their wives.

People didn't know where to place me, and I was a threat to their norms in many cases. Even when they didn't know that I was gay.

There were no role models in pop culture, I can tell you that. I felt like a first.

Advertisers just loved to portray men as bumbly-fumbly fools when it came to cooking, cleaning, or taking care of the kids. Brands loved to honor the mom as the ultimate caregiver, leaving the dad in the living room, sitting in his favorite chair, reading the paper and watching television. I was personally involved in making a lot of this advertising, so I knew firsthand. And there were very few active fathers depicted in entertainment; *Kramer vs. Kramer* was as much an anomaly as I was.

I can remember many photo shoots where we had to show the man with a wedding ring on his finger. Here I was a single gay father...yes, I felt the prejudice. Yet in a disturbing way, I was professionally contributing to it. But I couldn't stop it or say a word.

School and friends were one thing, but I also worried about losing clients. I anticipated that they'd be prejudiced against me once they heard I was gay. I was worried that their perceptions of me would flip on a dime once they found out about me.

Remember, this was the *Ellen* era. Advertisers were dropping her show left and right, including my biggest clients. It's hard to imagine now, but I remember it like it was yesterday. I remember the feeling of prejudice in the air whenever it came up at work.

I had been in many a conference room where there was gay bashing, with the "basher" not knowing who was sitting in the room.

As an agency person and "vendor" at the time, I sat there quietly because I was afraid to defend anything or anyone. I'm a bit embarrassed about that now.

I remember a guy I wanted to hire once who almost got blocked by senior management because he "seemed gay." So naturally I believed the same prejudice would be thrown on me too, once they found out that I was gay.

Oh, those poor kids.

Years later, an old colleague asked me to help with an LGBT task force at Johnson & Johnson, to which I gladly agreed. Times eventually started to change, and I was happy to see the progress and to be a part of it.

This was after I developed the very first print ad for Tylenol targeting gay men in 2003. It was a first for the brand, but Tylenol was also the first over-the-counter (OTC) healthcare product to show its "pride." It was a first for me too. I was so honored to have ownership of it. The ad, timed for Gay Pride Weekend in New York City, got a lot of press at the time, where I was described as not only the creator but as "openly gay."

"Openly gay"...definitely a first. Sounds so dated now.

With that Tylenol ad, I was out publicly for all my clients to know.

It's just not easy coming out. It's still not easy. I still meet people who are fearful of coming out.

I had to accept whatever would come with that "openly gay" label, despite the "don't ask, don't tell" environment we were living in. I know now, especially living in New York City, that this all seems so stupid and irrelevant. At the time, it was quite real, I'm sad to say.

There were a few folks where I did find solace: the very rare but amazing stay-at-home dad.

There were only a few back then, compared to now when it is much more common to see dad at home with their kids while mom is out working. At the time some of the dads still worked, but they held more flexible jobs so that they could take care of the kids. Others were full time homemakers in the traditional sense of the word, except that they were men.

I easily bonded with these guys, and they didn't seem to care that I was gay, if they even knew. They embraced me because I was a full time dad too, even took me out for coffee to chat a few times. They'd help me pick up the kids when schedules were tough, and I did the same for them. It was nice. While they never said it out loud these few guys respected me as a father, gay or not.

These stay-at-home dads "got" me, and I got them. We were all definitively in the minority, so I think we connected around it.

Active fatherhood is much more common now, if not the norm.

In my time, there just weren't many fathers like me active in their kids' school, and there were no "out" gay people like me at all. If they were around, they were invisible. I was alone.

If I had been a single mom, the scenario would have been quite different. Women's support networks were quite extensive and quite frankly they flaunted it.

#SGD? No such luck.

It really didn't matter in the end, though…I got through it. I just looked for support in other places…

CHAPTER 8
Finding New Hope

As you can probably imagine, New Hope became my social sanctuary and a place I would go to meet people and have a little fun.

I was still relatively young (especially as I look back), so the bar scene was fertile ground for meeting other gay men. I sought refuge in New Hope, hoping to find a place where I'd make friends who would understand and support me.

When you think about it, back then the only place any of us could go to meet other gay men was at a gay bar, whether you were looking to make friends, make a date, or just hang out. Everything happened at the gay bars. Restaurants and bars were nowhere near as mixed as they are today, so if I wanted to hang out with other gay men then I had to go to a gay bar.

It's funny how many of the gay bars in New Hope, and New York for that matter, are closing. I guess we don't need to congregate in our own place anymore; gay people are much more assimilated into mainstream culture now. It's a good thing, but those gay bars were special places back in the day.

On the surface, I was well received socially in New Hope, at least at first. I developed a nice group of casual friends that I would see when I went out. I wouldn't say any of them were close friends, but they were what we called "bar friends."

Honestly, I don't think a lot of people cared about getting to know me outside of the bars. I had kids and almost all of them did not, so I was an anomaly there in New Hope too, just like I was at the kids' school. My life was so different from others on both sides of my world.

I mean how many other gay men have this kind of schedule with kids and an ex-wife:

JOURNAL:
F 1/16 6:00pm – next morn
S 1/17 morn – 8:45am
Went to work at (my daughter's) school
2:30pm – next morn
Took (my daughter) to 1st haircut
Ran into (Mom) at The Cartwheel
S 1/18 morn – next morn

Most of the gay men I met couldn't relate to my "lifestyle," ironically, and they kept me at an arm's length as a result…fun to hang with at the bar, but not much beyond that.

I couldn't win either way!

Telling people I'd just met that I had kids was always such a mental debate for me – when do I drop that news? The kids were still very little and a handful at that – not exactly helpful for an active social life or dating. It wasn't like I could have people over to my place.

So I never really knew when to break the news to someone. I rarely mentioned the kids when I first met people, but then I would agonize over when I should say something. I had anxiety over it, to the point where sometimes I couldn't enjoy myself in anticipation of having to talk about it. It's not that I wasn't proud of the kids, it was my issue of not fitting in.

When I did say something, a lot of the time I didn't exactly get a positive reaction. Many of the gay men treated me like I had somehow sold out. Not sure how that's the case, but they acted like the fact that I got married to a woman made me somehow less gay. And the fact that I had two kids made me very unattractive…not to everyone, but to enough of them that it made me skittish.

While no one ever said anything to my face, it was all in gossip and in body language.

Picture this: a new friend invites you to a party at his apartment so that you can meet some other guys from town. At the party, he introduces you to a really nice, good-looking guy who you can't believe is single. He's that awesome. Even more awesome, he asks for your phone number after the two of you chat for almost an hour. After a few days of agonizingly waiting for the phone to ring (because he asked for your number, not vice versa), he calls you and asks you out. He says, "Let's meet for a drink first, and then decide where to go after that." You can't believe it, he's that good looking. The thought of sitting across a table from him is frightening, and the thought of where you'll go after that drink is exhilarating. He confirms again on the morning of the day you're going to meet, and you agonize over what to wear: which jeans look the best on you, should it be a t-shirt or collared shirt...every detail.

You meet him for the drink on a beautiful Saturday afternoon at an outdoor café, where lots of people are walking by. He looks even better than you remember, and you are thrilled that all these people are seeing you sitting with him. He's scrubbed clean for the date so he obviously put some care into getting ready. He's wearing amazing cologne that fills your imagination, and he's wearing a light blue shirt that not only matches his eyes but also fits just perfectly snug. He's got a smile as big as the sun, and so do you. This is going to be a great night.

While sipping drinks, you are both going back and forth asking the questions you ask on a first date. The body language is positive in every aspect, he's leaning forward, paying attention to every word you say, and that bright smile is still there with every question.

He even grabs your forearm while laughing at something you said.

Wow.

The conversation starts to go down a line where you really have to say that you have two little kids. If you don't say something now, it'll be odd later when you do say something. After all, you hadn't said anything at the party, and now it'll get weird if you don't bring it up naturally in the conversation. He'll think you were purposefully hiding it, which isn't the case. You wait and wait for the right moment, so that it doesn't come completely out of left field. The time feels right when he asks about your apartment so you say, "Well, I have two kids so I just recently moved to a new place that has two bedrooms."

He asks with disbelief, "You have kids?" You can see the wheels turning as he asks, "Did you adopt?"

Here go the line of questions. "Oh, you were married?"

Oh yes, I was married. In other words, yes I have baggage. A matched set actually.

Now feel this: the body language instantly changes. The alert, edge-of-his seat posture changes immediately as he leans back in his chair and folds his big arms. The smile is gone. Luckily for him, his drink is almost done so he can take the last swig and not have it be so obvious that he is trying to finish fast. He quickly leads the conversation to a close, as politely as he can, probably hoping that you're not noticing what he's trying to do.

He's trying to leave gracefully.

He says it was wonderful *(wonderful?)* grabbing a drink and he's sure he'll see you around. You are left there sitting alone at this outdoor table, everyone still walking by, looking at the empty seat right next to you. You're flipping a quarter back and forth, wondering how you could have avoided that interchange; wondering if this dating thing will ever work and wondering what you did wrong.

Rock, meet bottom.

I later heard from my friend who had the party that this guy just didn't want to deal with someone who was *just* coming out. But I had been out for over a year, so I didn't buy it.

What's more likely, and what was the more common judgment, was that he figured "I should have known" I was gay. Many gay men just simply thought that I must have known all along – I must have had an affair at some point along the way but just wasn't coming clean about it, and that I was a cop-out because I had kids. Or that because I had kids I was somewhat less "gay."

Either way, I had "issues."

Either way, I was certainly a whole lot less fun because I had kids. Not their fault, not "his" fault, but it made me very unappealing to many men, either for friends or for dating.

So be it.

You might be thinking that this was all in my head, but I knew this to be true because I had become friendly with a former work colleague who lived in my apartment complex. He told me straight up how it played out.

I had not seen him in years, certainly not since I had gotten divorced, but I did run into him at the Cartwheel one Saturday night in New Hope. It was an odd "what are you doing here" kind of moment. After that night, we started hanging out together from time to time, going to the clubs with each other so that we didn't have to stand at the bar alone.

He eventually opened up that he had carried a lot of animosity towards me when we were working together at J&J back when I was married.

He said that he could tell I was gay (not sure how) and it angered him that I had the fulfilled the dream: a wife and kids. He couldn't understand how I was able to do it, yet he hadn't been able to do the same thing. But on the flip side, he also felt like I had taken the easy way out by not confronting the fact that I was gay. He said he almost ignored me the night we ran into each other at the Cartwheel because he just felt like I was not the kind of person he wanted to be around.

He had a lot to say.

I didn't hang around with him too much after that, even though he was just being honest.

To this day I am still intrigued by how he knew I was gay, even before I did, just like my two New York work friends. Back then, most people looked at me and would have never thought I was gay, and here is this guy judging me because of what he assumed.

So while I did indeed have my bar friends, my path to find serenity in New Hope came very slowly. I eventually stopped trying to assemble a posse of friends and I focused more on just dating. I wanted a boyfriend. I wanted to find someone to spend my life with. I wanted love.

Boyfriend? Love? Too heavy?

When I was in college, I saw the amazing Linda Ronstadt in concert. When she arrived on campus for her gig, she went to one of the sororities and borrowed a Cornell cheerleading outfit to wear on stage. She stood still at the microphone, in a Big Red cheerleading uniform, and sang one of the most haunting yet beautiful songs I had ever heard, *Desperado*. It was a moment.

I wanted to *be* her, in that cheerleading outfit, singing into that microphone.

No, I didn't know I was gay.

I thought of that moment, her moment, many times through the years, especially when I was feeling a bit down on the dating scene.

There is nothing better than live music whether you are in a concert venue that holds thousands or a small cabaret that holds only a hundred…live music takes you away. I always relate to the lyrics. I guess it's the writer in me.

As an aside, you have not lived until you've heard live Donna Summer sing *Last Dance*, The Who sing *Eminence Front*, Whitney Houston sing *The Greatest Love of All*, The Rolling Stones sing *Under My Thumb*, and Linda Ronstadt sing *Desperado*.

> *It may be raining, but there's a rainbow above you*
> *You better let somebody love you, before it's too late*

I felt like *Desperado* most days…I'd been "out riding fences for so long now."

I wanted someone in New Hope to love me.

I tried very hard not to let the turkeys get me down, I really did. I put most of my focus on the kids and on work, and dated when the opportunity came along and felt right. I've always been really good at focusing.

There would be far less judgment if I did that, or so I hoped.

I was working on what became the biggest prescription to over-the-counter (OTC) product launch in history, Pepcid AC. It kept me very busy. My agency worked on *all* of the promotional materials and *all* of the retail displays that *all* had to hit stores on *exactly* the same day, *exactly* when the FDA said that it could be available for sale at retail.

It required a lot of resources and a lot of coordination.

I had plenty to do.

I knew that eventually I'd make new friends and maybe even meet someone special. I figured it would happen, so I would just have to enjoy the process as best I could. In the meantime, my focus would be the kids and work, in priority order.

Patience is a virtue, or so I told myself.

But boy, it was not easy, that's for sure, despite the parade of men…

CHAPTER 9

Flags and Stickers

Aside from December, June is my favorite month of the year. I just love December and the holiday season, for all the decorations, parties, and family time.

But I also love June because it's Gay Pride Month.

When you're in New York City, especially around The Village, Chelsea, or Hell's Kitchen, the city comes alive during Pride Month. The restaurants, bars, and shops all put up Pride flags…you see a complete buffet of rainbows as you walk down the streets. It makes me so happy for a variety of reasons, not the least of which is the public recognition of acceptance. I hadn't acknowledged myself for years, so you can imagine how good it feels to see Pride so abundant, and the acceptance so abundant.

But the real reason I love seeing all those rainbow flags flying so proudly is because it reminds me of my first Gay Pride weekend in 1997. My son had recently turned two and I felt like I was the one being born again!

I had gone on a couple of dates with this guy I met at the Cartwheel in New Hope, and he seemed like a good guy. He really understood how much I wanted to get into the community, so he opened his arms and his friends to me, which was so sweet.

It was June, and when I told him that I'd never been to Gay Pride, he seized the opportunity.

He was determined to make my first Gay Pride experience a special one, so we started out with drinks at his neighbor's apartment before heading into the city. He wanted to make sure that I met his friends before hopping in a car with them.

They were such a welcoming crowd; it felt so good. A few of them asked me about the kids, but in a way that showed real interest, not just gossip mongering. They seemed to love that I was a dad.

We piled into his car to drive the hour and a half into New York, all of us excited for the day ahead. I knew it was going to be a special day when we stopped at a rest area and the woman at the sunglass counter gave me a free pair of sunglasses because I was "part of the family." How did she know?

Gay pride, I guess!

When we got into the city, we planted ourselves in front of the Stonewall Inn, the original bar where Pride started decades ago. I hadn't heard the history before, so they schooled me on the way in. I got a lesson in Pride on I-95 in New Jersey.

The vantage point for the parade could not have been better, right near the corner of Christopher Street and Seventh Avenue where the crowds would surely be the thickest. He wanted me to have the whole experience. Every time someone questioned why we were doing something, he would say, "Because this is Jim's first Pride." With that, everyone obliged.

The location proved quite fruitful for a few reasons, not the least of which because it was hotter than hot that day. We could go into the Stonewall Inn to have a drink but not get lost in the crowd or lose our spot on the parade route. We'd run in, have a beer and dance to a couple of songs, and then run back out to see more of the parade.

At one point, I had gone in with him to grab a beer and he went over to the DJ who was spinning the best dance music I have ever heard. The place was jumping up and down to the beat. It looked like he was putting in a request.

Suddenly the song *I Am What I Am* by Gloria Gaynor came on, and the whole crowd lit up. Our little group formed a circle and started singing along to the song. Well, shouting is probably more accurate, but you get the picture.

Halfway through, he said to me, "This is your first Pride, and I wanted you to experience this." It was one of the sweetest things that anyone ever did for me, with perfect timing.

Actually the entire day couldn't have been more perfect. I was proud to be gay. Finally? Maybe.

Hours went by as we waited in anticipation for the parade to come to us. We were right by a major turn in the route so waiting to see the first glimpse of the marchers was like waiting for Santa on Christmas. The parade was always led by a bunch of women on motorcycles, so you could hear the parade coming for a block or so.

When it finally started to turn the corner and we heard the roar of the engines, I had another one of those overwhelming moments like the first time I went to Splash.

I suddenly noticed, for the first time that day, the immense sea of people and the abundance of waving rainbow flags. Miraculously the entire street was completely alive and in full rainbow color.

I had never seen so many gay people in one place in my entire life. I didn't even know there were that many gay people in New York!

It was also the first time I witnessed the diversity in gay people. There were very few of the stereotypes most people held, but instead every size, shape, form, color, and texture you could possibly imagine.

They were all walking or watching with Pride, Gay Pride.

I mentioned to him how I had never seen anything like this in my life, and he beamed in response. Mission accomplished. Luckily, I had sunglasses on to hide the stream of teams running down my face. Pure joy. Scratch that, pure Pride.

So that's why I love the weeks leading up to Gay Pride Weekend in New York so much. That's why every year I have to see at least a glimpse of the parade, and go to at least one bar to have a drink and hear some dance music. Those flags of acceptance still make me beam, as do the memories of my first Gay Pride.

I was so proud to be gay. Finally!

Now juxtapose that parade with another one that I didn't personally experience, but that my kids did: the Pro-Life March on Washington.

The kids were young, very young, and in Catholic grade school.

I quietly nodded along when my daughter told me that she was missing a day of school to go to the March for Life with her mom and her little brother. She actually called it "The March," as if I would know exactly what it was.

Maybe I should have, but I didn't know much about it. But I was about to find out.

I had a voicemail to pick them up at 7:00pm when the bus would get back to the school from Washington. There was no explanation, just a request to pick them up on time. They had slept at their mom's house the night before since the bus was leaving so early in the morning.

As I sat in the parking lot of the school, waiting anxiously for the bus to come, I couldn't imagine what I would hear from the kids. I knew of some things: marching, chanting, posters of hideous pictures. I was a bit worried about what they had likely witnessed that day, but I couldn't be sure one way or the other.

Of course the bus was late, and it was dark, which made the waiting and the anticipation even worse. I just remember sitting in my car in silence, no radio playing, waiting to see the school bus turn the corner. Finally, an hour or so later, I saw the headlights come down the street.

When the children, my children, jumped off the bus and came running to me, I saw odd patches on their coats that I didn't recognize from a distance. As they got closer I realized that those weren't patches, but pro-life stickers – a whole bunch of them, plastered on my young children like they were advertising billboards.

I tried so hard to mask the expression on my face. This was one for the journal, and for the lawyer.

I didn't talk to their mom, I just scooped them up into the car and took off while the other parents hung around chatting. I didn't care to engage.

As we drove home, I asked the kids to peel off the stickers. They thought I was concerned about the stickers ruining their coats; they didn't understand my real concern.

When we got home, I tried to probe them on what they had seen, but they didn't offer much detail. It's so typical of kids not to tell you about their day. I could rarely get anything out of them.

"What did you do in school today?" I would ask almost every day. "Nothing," was always the response. Other parents would say that they heard the same from their kids. Must be part of being a kid, I suppose.

I realized that they were too young to really know what they saw, and that it was just a big social event for them. But this was not their last "March," as they got older they certainly understood the and then I had to address head-on how I felt about the topic.

This was one for the Supreme Court, not me.

As Dad, I'm responsible for their emotional wellbeing, which includes equipping them to make their own decisions. I felt compelled to make sure they understood both sides of the argument, but I waited until they were old enough to comprehend it all and decide for themselves.

At that young age, I felt that they were too ill-equipped to have to deal with such sensitive issues, but I also felt like I had no choice but to go along with it. Maybe I should have made it a bigger deal at the time, I will never know.

I kept my mouth shut. Don't ask, don't tell.

As for the guy who brought me to my first Gay Pride, things ultimately didn't work out with him. It probably could have, but it didn't. I just wasn't ready. I felt bad for him because even though he was much younger than me, he was ready. His friends weren't so cool about it; they ignored me after I called it quits. We had only dated a few times, so I expected them to still be friendly to me, but that wasn't the case.

Which is exactly why I was very cautious about dating and letting people into my life. I didn't allow many people to meet the kids, including him. Just a few. I didn't want to engage at that level until I thought I might be ready, and I didn't want the kids to get excited and attached to someone who might not be around for long.

Now this had nothing to do with being gay; this was just being a proper parent, in my book. I don't think kids should witness a string of people coming in and out of their lives, which, let's face it, is exactly what happens when any of us are dating.

We are experimenting to see what we like, learning about what we are looking for, and trying to find what will make us happy. You have to kiss a lot of frogs to get the prince. My ex-wife was doing the same thing; I met a lot of them.

This is true whether you are gay or straight, male or female. I wasn't going to make a mistake finding the right partner this time around, so I was much more purposeful than when I was younger. I do try to learn from life along the way.

And while I said I wasn't ready, I was searching for someone to really make a connection. It got discouraging at times when I didn't think it would ever happen, but then I'd get a glimmer of hope from a date that would get me really excited and would re-energize me to keep trying. I knew I'd be ready when the right one came along.

One fun date, even if it was only one, gave me the strength to keep looking until I found the right guy. One good night would make me realize that he was out there, somewhere.

Sure enough, there he was in a pair of khaki shorts…

CHAPTER 10

The Top of the Stairs

It took some time, but I eventually got more and more involved in the community in New Hope.

I met some friends and starting doing what a single guy would do, SGD or not.

I had a couple short romances along the way with guys who were wonderful people, and they were completely supportive of me being a dad. There was nothing wrong with any of them; it's just that none of them were "The One."

I really do believe that things happen for a reason, so even if the person you are meeting in that moment isn't going to be in your life, they may lead to someone who will.

Bingo.

One night at a bar called the Raven in New Hope, I met an artist. How did I know he was an artist? Well, aside from looking the part and giving off that artist vibe, he literally had paint on his painter pants. Paint marks that don't come from painting houses, but from painting paintings.

He was entirely, 100%, not my type, but for some reason I was drawn to him at least for a short time. All he talked about was sex, and all the positions he liked. He was clearly a player, having been around the block a few times. Hell, I think he owned the block. None of that was important to me.

He asked me out and I was curious enough to take a bite. Well, I didn't bite, but you know what I mean. I'm really glad I did, because he led me to someone very special.

We only went on two dates, and that was it. After I was left sitting alone at that outdoor café that time, I started a rule that I tried to abide by: everyone gets two dates. You just can't tell enough about a person from one date so I always gave a budding relationship at least a second chance. So he got a second date, but that was it; there was no connection between us.

But I am very happy for that second date because that's when he introduced me to his friend, Christopher. It was a simple, casual hello, and that was it. A week or so later, I saw Christopher again, and we exchanged another simple, casual hello.

No big deal, not yet anyway. I thought he was insanely good looking, but didn't think about it other than that.

Then just a few weeks later, I was back at the Raven in New Hope with a couple friends for Sunday Tea. Sunday afternoon happy hour, or Sunday Tea, is the "gay happy hour" in pretty much every major city. New Hope was no exception. Sunday Tea is where I met the artist, and now this Sunday Tea was about to change my life forever.

It was a gorgeous summer day, and we were hanging out on the patio. It was definitely on the hot side, but that was okay because it made the view so much better: short shorts and tight t-shirts.

Fine by me.

As fate would have it, Christopher walked by and said another casual hello. I said hello back and he kept walking.

"Who is that?" said my friend. I mentioned that he was a friend of the artist.

"He's cute."

I agreed, but didn't go any further. I had been dating enough lately, and had decided that I was going to take a break. I was tired of thinking about it so much. I was tired of the dating cycle, the dating routine, and constantly waiting for phone calls and voicemails to see if someone was interested. I was tired of it all.

I was just going to focus on my newfound friends, work, and the kids. That's it. That's what I kept telling myself. That was more than enough.

My friends pushed and pushed me to go talk to Christopher, but I just wasn't up to it. They wouldn't let it go. "Hey you," they shouted over to him.

"You with the gorgeous legs and the banana boat smile."

Oh jeez; but they were right.

I think Christopher tried to ignore it at first, but my friends were persistent. Finally, Christopher walked over, drink in hand and big, banana boat smile intact.

"Not sure how I should respond," he said with his big, beaming smile. He had me at that smile, and the legs weren't so bad either. My friends do have good taste.

We all chatted for a few minutes, and then moved along our separate ways. It was nothing too dramatic, except that my one friend wouldn't let it go. I had come to really trust him and his partner. He was the one who defended me at that fateful dinner party where I was humiliated.

I had also had a very special "first" experience with this friend as well.

Now, while I will admit that there was a lot about being gay that came pretty easy to me, there is one thing I just couldn't ever imagine doing with another guy: slow dancing. I just couldn't imagine doing it. How do you hold hands? Where do you put the other hand? I mean, who leads?

I had gone with a date and a group of friends, including this friend, to a charity event a year earlier for a local AIDS fundraiser. It was an auction with tons of food, an open bar, and an amazing band. I watched with awe as I saw couples of gay men slow dancing. By this point I had been to many a dance club, so the sight of two gay men dancing was natural.

But slow dancing? I couldn't process that.

My friend must have seen me watching, thought that I wanted to dance, and asked me to take a twirl.

I replied, "There's no way I can do that. No way."

My response was like a challenge to this friend. I think in some ways he figured it was his duty; he was that kind of guy.

So slow dance we did, but I'm not sure that he'd ever ask me again. I stepped on his toes, I stumbled over my own feet, and couldn't quite grasp his big hands gracefully.

I don't remember the song that was playing, but I do remember how amazingly awkward yet wonderful it was, all at the same time. To this day, we joke about how I had my first slow dance with him. My first twirl, so to speak.

This is the same man who now gets so emotional whenever I talk about my kids being grown up. He follows their activity on Facebook.

So of course, when given the situation to hook me up with a good-looking guy, he wasn't going to let the chance go by. He playfully interacted with Christopher a few times that day, while I acted the part of shy and coy – although it wasn't just an act.

Nothing really big happened that day at Sunday Tea at the Raven, but it wasn't the last of Christopher either. Not by a long shot.

The following weekend one of my best friends from college was in town, so we decided to go to Philadelphia to a club called Shampoo. Friday night was "gay night," and it was *the* place for us to go. I got my regular babysitter who was old enough to drive, so I could have some fun with my old friend and the friend she was bringing along. It was going to be a night out, and I needed it after the week I'd had at work.

It was August of 1998, and it felt like I was getting ready to start a new semester of school.

A few days earlier, I had quit my job and announced that I was starting my own agency. It was a big leap for me. While it was time for me to move on and advance my career, it was also a highly emotional decision because I had come to really enjoy working with the team I had built and the clients I had secured.

It had been a roller coaster of a week so Friday night couldn't have come fast enough.

Shampoo had several dance floors, including a little side room where they played classic disco music. That's where we hung out most of the time.

The dance floor was packed that night, with guys and girls boogying up a storm. We took turns running to the bar so that we wouldn't lose our spots dancing.

As luck would have it, Christopher was also there.

He came up and said hello, so of course I introduced him to my friend who had just jumped down from the elevated box where she was twirling around. She wanted in on the conversation with this cute guy.

That's what friends are for.

This time it wasn't just that casual hello as he walked by; he seemed like he wanted to stay and talk.

We joked about seeing each other at the Raven, and how persistent my friends had been – a perfect icebreaker. Thank you, overly eager friends!

My old college friend quickly became like a dog with a bone. She wouldn't let him go. She kept telling me how cute he was, how nice he seemed, and how I needed to be more aggressive. She was thrilled when later I showed her the piece of paper with his number written on it. He wanted me to give him a call!

My friend and I danced the rest of the night, right down to the last dance to *Last Dance*.

I need you by me
Beside me to guide me

I went home feeling full of love from my friend, and full of hope from seeing Christopher.

I called him the next day. I wasn't going to play any of the games once played on me. Not with this one. My friend said that I needed to be more aggressive. I follow orders: I've established that.

I don't know what possessed me, but I invited him over to my apartment for dinner. I never did that! But I couldn't afford a babysitter two nights in a row, and I couldn't afford to go to a restaurant for dinner. And I couldn't afford to let too much time go by before I saw him again. He seemed interested, so I didn't want his interest to fade.

So I invited him over for dinner.

Shit.

My friends who know me now laugh their asses off when I tell the story, as does Christopher. Well, actually he just shakes his head.

I can't cook to save my life. Even my kids talk about how I can only cook four things: grilled cheese, lasagna (my specialty), pasta, and chicken stir-fry – and none of them very well. Actually, my lasagna is to die for.

I made chicken stir-fry that night, right out of the freezer bag.

Because I didn't really let many people meet the kids, I told him to come over at 8:30pm. At this point, my kids were on a highly regimented schedule, so they were in bed and asleep by 7:30 at night, without fail.

By having him come at 8:30pm, this would give me time to get the kids fed, bathed, and in bed with plenty of time to spare. Time enough to cook the chicken stir-fry, and primp myself a little.

One thing that made this all so much easier is that I never had to go through the awkward moment of telling Christopher about the kids. He already knew from the artist. Check that off the list. But still, he'd only meet the kids when I was good and ready.

After one year in my first apartment, I had moved into a two-bedroom apartment that I totally couldn't afford, but the kids needed a room of their own. Sharing a bedroom just wasn't healthy for them or for me, and they were with me several nights a week and every weekend. They needed their space and so did I.

The apartment was on the second floor of a brand new complex, but the front door was on the first floor, which made for a strange layout. So when you entered the apartment, you had to immediately walk up a flight of stairs, which landed right in front of the kids' bedroom.

While the format wasn't ideal, everything was new and it was far more spacious than the dump I was previously in.

I loved the kids' bedroom the most because my parents helped me get the coolest bunk beds – the top bed had a single mattress for my daughter while the bottom bed was a double for my son, making it so much safer. Plus, now my sister had a place to sleep when she would visit from Boston.

My sister always slept with the kids when she visited; it was her way of bonding with them. I don't think this was much of a sacrifice except for the one Easter she was visiting us. My son had decided to hide his Easter candy so that no one else could eat it. I guess he figured a safe place would be his aunt's sleeping bag. I also guess he forgot where he had hidden the candy because the next morning my poor sister woke up all covered in chocolate from rolling back and forth across countless chocolate Easter eggs all night.

Whoops. I don't think I laughed so hard in my life.

But I digress.

I always worried about those stairs, though, for their safety. So I installed a gate at the top so that if they were playing or sleepwalking, they couldn't accidently fall down. The installed gate made for a relaxed dad.

The night that Christopher came over, everything was running according to plan. I was super excited about him coming over, and I wanted the night to be perfect.

I fed the kids pasta, gave them baths, and got them to bed, right on schedule. I got all the food ready and took a shower myself, with plenty of time to spare. I put on a pair of jeans and a colorful shirt, trying to look like I thought about it but not that I obsessed about it either.

Not a peep from the kids, just like every other night.

At about 8:35pm, Christopher knocked on the door and I slowly and quietly moved around the gate and walked down the stairs to let him in. I wasn't trying to be quiet because the kids were sound sleepers, but I didn't want him to hear me rushing.

Hell no.

He walked in the door and gave me a quick hug. I closed the door behind him and there standing at the top of the stairs, right at the gate, were the kids.

"Oh, hi, guys!"

I can see it now, like it just happened. They were both in one-piece pajamas, the ones with feet on them. My son's were blue, and my daughter's were red, because at that time these were their favorite colors.

They were standing at the top of the stairs, waiting to meet the person who was coming through the door. It was the cutest, most amazing view I had ever seen, and such foreshadowing for what was to come.

The universe sends us signs, and this was a sign. My kids were telling me to relax; they were telling me to stop worrying; they were telling me that they were supporting me.

I shrugged my shoulders as if to say "whatever," and we walked up the stairs together.

I introduced them to Christopher; he shook both of their hands. Those handshakes, looking back, were so symbolic of his relationship with them. He didn't assume anything, even in that first interaction.

Right after they said hello, they jumped back into bed and we didn't hear from them again all night. They didn't bug me to stay up; they were just excited to see who had come over.

Christopher ate my dinner gracefully, which was noble of him. I could only hope that the company and the conversation more than made up for any weaknesses in the kitchen.

After talking on the couch for a few hours, he asked if I would walk him to his car. As we approached his silver Volkswagen convertible, he popped the trunk and took out the largest bouquet of all white flowers I have ever seen. Little did he know that white flowers are my absolute favorite. There's just something about the purity of them.

He said that he didn't want to give them to me earlier, in case the kids were still up. How thoughtful, insightful...mature. I couldn't believe it.

It was August 9th, 1998 and as I walked back up those stairs I couldn't help but contemplate what might come next. I climbed into bed alone, but not feeling alone at all.

Sure we had a great evening, but would he ever call me again…

CHAPTER 11

Working Together

The next day, he called me! Early.

There were no games, no teasing, no built-up anticipation. He was making it known that he was interested, so I took it. I was a bit skeptical, for no other reason than my prior experiences, but I said that I'd love to meet for dinner the next Saturday night.

I reminded myself that everyone always gets two dates.

I thought about him the entire next day, and all week long for that matter. I felt like a teenager, anxious to go to the Prom on Saturday.

Little did I know that August 9th would become our anniversary date and that we'd end up celebrating it year after year. But at the time I was just being realistic.

It was one date, and we really didn't do anything. I had experienced other first dates before too, and they didn't go anywhere. I cooked an awful dinner and we talked on the couch. That was it. We had a long way to go and Saturday seemed a long way away. I still had an entire week of work and kids to get through.

Hey, I was starting a new agency and I had a lot of work ahead of me.

He told me to meet him at Judy's, a very "gay" restaurant in Philadelphia that I had been to before with friends before a night of dancing at Shampoo. There weren't many gay-friendly restaurants back then, so Judy's was a hot spot. It was familiar territory and equal distance for both of us, since he lived in Delaware at the time.

When I walked in the restaurant, he was already at the bar chit-chatting with the woman sitting next to him. I actually thought he knew her, but turns out that he was just being friendly. I eventually found out that he does that everywhere he goes; tonight was no different.

I joined them at the bar for a glass of wine, and when we finished we sat down at a small table. While the place was packed, loud, and consumed by live music, it was as if we were the only two people in the room. We had complete tunnel vision, in a total vacuum, hanging on to each other's every word. It's like there was a cone put around us to shut out the rest of the restaurant.

He had shorts on (yes, there were those legs again), and a green linen shirt that matched his eyes. We talked and talked and talked, until we were the last ones in the restaurant. When we finally lifted our heads and looked around, the staff was putting the chairs up on tables for the night.

His car was parked a lot farther away than mine so I drove him to his parking lot and we chatted a bit more. It was amazing.

While everyone got a second date, this one turned into a whole lot more than that. We soon found ourselves going out every weekend without fail. We got to the point that it became almost automatic.

I didn't hide the kids, and I certainly felt very comfortable talking about them, but they really didn't know Christopher yet. It was time to have them all spend a little time together. We were starting to get serious, so I was open to the idea.

Was I ready? I was ready to accept that maybe *this* is "the one." I was ready to accept that maybe he should get to know the kids and vice versa.

One weekend I decided we'd all go to the Philadelphia Aquarium – that way we'd all get to do something together, something that the kids would really like. It was a Sunday and Christopher was working on a jobsite downtown, so we met him there before going to the aquarium.

At the time, Christopher was an interior landscaper, which basically meant he designed how to fill an interior space with plantings, flowers, decorations, etc. His clients were businesses that owned office buildings, malls, airports… any kind of open public space that needs interior plant-scaping to make it attractive and inviting. Holidays were the busiest time of the year as you can imagine, when every business in town is decking the halls.

That week, he was re-imagining an open interior space in a downtown Philadelphia office building, and had to do a site check.

When we arrived, Christopher was standing high above a palm tree in a raised electronic ladder. This, of course, made him an instant hero with my son. Check.

After he was done with the site inspection, we spent the rest of the day at the aquarium, looking at sharks and eating lunch. It was so nice to be out with the kids and a date, and not feel at all self-conscious. I wasn't worried about him meeting them, and I wasn't worried about what they would think. We were all just being.

I knew it had gone well when my daughter asked if Christopher could come home with us. I didn't want to push it too much that day – we had to give the man some time to get used to even being with kids. We parted ways in Philadelphia.

I don't know how to say it, but it all just worked. We progressed along very naturally, but also very quickly. It was just right. It's interesting how your body and mind can expand to the capacity you need it, because at the exact same time I met Christopher, I had decided to put a hold on dating and to just focus on my new business. I felt like work needed all the energy I could muster, and I was over the dating drama for a while.

Bam, enter Christopher!

Job, home, kids, and relationship were all starting to work together. I was starting to just "be" for the first time since college.

Because everything was working together so well, Christopher and I started talking about making this whole thing more of a "thing." I was ready to make it more, and so was he.

We didn't want to live in my current apartment, though, because for a couple and two kids there just wasn't enough room and enough privacy. We could have made it work, but we had two incomes so we could upgrade to something more appropriate for what would now be four of us.

We talked a lot about where we'd want to live, and what we'd want out of a house. The planning and the talking was the best part. The kids were still very young, so a move wasn't something they'd quite understand, although we did talk about it with them.

They started to get excited, but I wasn't really sure they knew what they were getting excited about. We both had our parents in the loop too, who all nodded along in agreement. They were all just happy to see us all happy.

As Christopher and I started to talk about how we might make this all work, we decided to move to New Hope. We bought a small condo along the Delaware River, within walking distance to town along a historic canal. The condo was built from an old paper mill, so the views of the river rapids were breathtaking. That view never got old and I will never forget it.

We liked the layout because our bedroom was upstairs completely separate, while the kids' bedroom was on the first floor right off of the kitchen and living room. It was a great little home and fit us just right. We have a lot of fond memories from living there.

It brought us all a lot of hope for our future as a family.

My son still says it was his favorite place.

From day one our home was always filled with flowers, amazing bouquets that Christopher would artfully create from stuff he either brought home from work or bought at the store.

I also quickly found out that Christopher was an amazing cook. Thank goodness. His specialty was anything delicious, made from the hardest to find ingredients. I rarely stepped into a grocery store or stood behind the stove again. When I did, it was to run out for a few missing ingredients that were impossible for me to find (I'm a klutz at the grocery store too) or to chop up vegetables or slice a loaf of French bread.

Ironically, at the time I was doing the marketing for the first online grocery store, Netgrocer.com, the precursor to Peapod. I was developing creative concepts to motivate consumers to buy groceries from a website, which couldn't be more perfect for me. I could relate to the convenience.

Our division of household labor worked out well because I am a master at laundry and doing the dishes. We both did the cleaning. We completely shared domestic responsibilities, and he never had a problem when I had to focus on the kids. "This is how it's supposed to be," I would say to myself in disbelief, recognizing how much my life had changed.

Christopher and I were working together to make a home, which was something new and exciting for me. Working together with the kids.

Let me tell you, the kids noticed it too. They loved his food, and they often cooked with him. I think they also felt my happiness too. Kids can absolutely sense what's going on with their parents.

Every few weeks we would have a taco night, where he would spread out all the ingredients and the kids would make their own meal. What a delicious mess! Grated cheese, tomatoes, and shredded lettuce everywhere! After the first night of that, I quickly learned to put a sheet under the table for easier cleanup. Fool me once…

They never questioned why Christopher was living with us, why he didn't have his own bedroom, or why there were two men in the house. They accepted it partly because I think they were so young and didn't even know to question it. They also accepted it because it was working, so there was nothing to question.

We were working together.

Others certainly questioned it, and commented on it, but none of us did. I felt a confidence that I hadn't experienced in a long time. I didn't care what people thought; I only cared that we were happy.

Even when the kids' mom asked me to have Christopher sleep on the couch, I said no. I was starting to stand up for myself, which was a good thing, although I was still very careful. I never said no, or yes for that matter, without documenting it in my journal and checking with my lawyer.

JOURNAL 1/22
As far as sleeping, I told her no, that I was in a committed, permanent life relationship and that's how I lived my life with my kids. I was going to only be honest and that I would never expose them to anything that would be alarming to them.

I decided to call the lawyer to get some advice.

I tried as best I could to keep Christopher out of any of the drama or any of the heavy lifting with the kids.

The kids were still early risers, so I would get up at 6:00am on weekend mornings and play Candy Land with them in their room, until a more suitable time for Christopher to wake up. If you've ever played that game, you know how hateful Queen Frostine is. She's evil because she makes the game go on forever! My son would cry and cry when he got Queen Frostine. "I hate that woman," he would say, as his face would get beet red. He was so cute!

Then he would quickly rebound and ask "Can we wake up Christopher now?"

"Let him sleep," I would say. Now the tides have turned and it's Christopher asking if he can go wake up our son when he's home from college!

"Let him sleep," I still say, in true role reversal!

Looking back I can't believe how good Christopher was about it all.

> *Imagine this*: You are twenty-nine, you're a gay man, and you've fallen in love. But he has two children who are with him almost all of the time. You quickly fall into a groove with the man. But most of the time you're together, the kids are with you too. To go out, he has to hire a babysitter so you stay in quite a bit. While you love this man, you're not quite sure how you fit in. You clearly are not going to attempt to be the kids' father, because they already have one. And you clearly are not going to attempt to be their mother, because you are a man and they already have a mom. So what are you? What do the kids call you? How do you describe your relationship? Does this mean that you now have kids too, or are they just "his" kids? As a father, he has a clearly defined role in the household, but what's yours?

For Christopher, that was a lot to figure out in a new relationship, and for me that was a lot of responsibility to bring into a new relationship. We were working on it together.

While I had been taking a "go with the flow" attitude toward scheduling nights and weekends with the kids, we eventually had to spell out a more regular plan, because it was just getting too hard to manage, for their mom as well as for us. The older the kids, the more complicated the scheduling.

We had the kids almost every weekend in the beginning, as well as many nights during the week. We took it day by day with their mom, which was fine when they were younger and when I was single, but it was getting tougher by the week as they got older. Plus they needed a more regular schedule too.

Their mom and I both agreed to try to set a schedule ahead of time, so that we could all plan better. Of course, every time we set a plan it would have to change for one reason or another.

I had my own business now. While it did put more demands on me, it also allowed a flexible enough schedule for dealing with the constant variations in nights and weekends that just naturally occurred.

The new agency was doing quite well, and in fact, I recouped all the start-up costs within the first six months. My very first assignment was to re-design the packaging for Dentyne Ice chewing gum. The snow-capped mountains had to be placed just right next to the new logo. I got paid $1,000 to do the layouts, and that job became my first framed one-dollar bill for my little agency. There were many more to come, thankfully!

It was a constant juggling act of conflicting calendars that were getting more and more complicated, putting my administrative skills to the test as we balanced everyone's needs: the kids, the mom, Christopher, the agency, and mine. Wow!

I would photocopy endless calendars, fill out the nights and weekends, and give a copy to their mom, all so we could make sure we were in synch. As soon as we got a flow down, something would change. She was amazingly co-operative about it, I must say, as the schedule fluctuated back and forth.

Once the kids were both in school fulltime and started having their own schedule of activities, it added another layer on top of our endless scheduling demands. Their calendar trumped any of ours, and I was fortunate to have a job where I could let that happen. I always worked around it.

The beginning of each school year was always the roughest, getting settled in and prepared for the semesters ahead.

There was always a big hurdle to overcome, every single new school year…

CHAPTER 12
You Look Like You Need A Hug

I've always dreaded the first day of school.

Sure, "Jim Joseph" sounds like a cool name; I've been told there's a bit of a Hollywood feel to it. But when your formal name is James John Joseph III, it's an entirely different story.

At most schools, official registrations always go by your formal name, so every single year, without fail, the new teacher would call out my name slowly and clearly: James John Joseph The Third.

While it was a name that gave my grandmother great pride, it was perfect fodder for ridicule in my grade school years.

Rarely would any of the teachers get it right on the first day. They'd get the order of the names wrong, they'd make a comment about "the third," or they'd comment something absolutely humiliating that always made the first day of school every year just an absolute disaster for me.

James John Joseph III.

The kids in class would chuckle, and I'd never hear the end of it. "The turd" would inevitably come out at some point. I would sit and try to think of ways to avoid the same experience every year, but I could never prevent the trauma. I learned to just grin and bear it.

I would beg my mother to register me under "Jim," but I don't think she had a choice. It would take me days to get over it. To this day I always refer to myself as "Jim" just to avoid the whole first-name-last-name thing. My bank accounts say "Jim," and even most of my credit cards.

It's gotten a little trickier with newer Homeland Security regulations, so now all my travel documents read James John Joseph. Takes me right back to second grade every time I board a flight!

Which is why I had so much patience with my son on his first day of school every year.

My son had horrible separation anxiety, every single year on that first day – in fact, generally for the whole first week of school every fall. It started right with Pre-K, despite the fact that he would beg and beg to go to school when his older sister started going. When it was his turn, though, it was very tough for him to leave the nest.

"I don't want to go, I don't want to go," he would cry and cry.

As a result, I tried to make back-to-school an event to celebrate. We'd start getting ready a few weeks ahead with new shoes, sneakers, and clothes, and we'd start to plan out our schedules. We'd make a big trip to Staples to get organized with new school supplies, backpacks, and lunch boxes. It was a lot of fun, and every year we'd make it a big celebration even though it broke the bank.

I would have done anything to make that first day easier.

Every year on the first day, I would make a big sign with their names on it and bring balloons to the bus stop. During the early years, the kids loved it. Of course, as they got older they started to get embarrassed. I didn't care; I kept it up until my daughter finished eighth grade and then I had no choice but to stop. She would have killed me if I did it to her going into high school!

To this day, each kid has a photo album with a picture of the first day of school labeled with the years. It chronicles their childhood, grade after grade.

My daughter would march immediately onto the bus, and wave from the window as I waved the sign I had made. Then I'd fight back the tears as I hopped into my car to drive to work.

I tried to be there on the first day when they'd come home from school too, at least the first few years. I wasn't always as successful given work demands, but I tried.

My daughter always embraced the first day of school, with her new backpack filled with crayons, tape, a glue stick, and a ruler. For the life of me I don't know why we always bought little staplers too, but we did.

But it wasn't that way with my son, not at all.

Every year he would freak out on the first day. He would cry and hold tight with all his little might to avoid getting on the bus. That was always the first hurdle, getting on the bus. We'd inevitably miss it because he was too upset. I'd have to wave the driver off without us and then drive him to school, hoping that he'd calm down by the time we got there.

Every year I would hope that this would be the year that he had gotten over it, only to be faced with the trauma again when dropping him off.

It was like me hoping this would be the year that my teacher would call me "Jim" on the first day. Well not this year, but maybe next year.

The kids went to a very small, Catholic grade school (too small in my opinion), where everyone knew everyone else and where the principal and school administrators got to know us (and me) very well.

There was no mystery about me, especially at this point, and they were incredibly supportive.

They also knew that we faced separation anxiety with my son every year, because they had seen it year in and year out – so they would try to be around to help. They would try coming out to the car to say hello first, or they'd stand waiting at the door to greet him; but trust me when I say that nothing made it easier for my son.

One year in particular, we were on day three of the school year and I was still having trouble getting him to school without a lot of upset. After having missed the bus again, I pulled up to the school, and I swear as soon as they saw my car, the two ladies were standing in the door.

I turned the car off and my son immediately started to cry. I would ask him why he was crying, and he would respond, "I don't know." I would reason with him that I have to go to work anyway, to which he would respond with either "I'll wait for you," or "I'll come with you," or "I'm going to miss you."

It broke my heart, every time.

I finally got him to calm down enough to get him out of the car, and as we were walking to the door he started to cry again. I knelt down to be at eye level with him and just hugged him until he calmed down. I looked at him right in the eye and told him that he just had to go to school if he ever wanted to have a job like his dad. I told him how much I loved having him come to my office, and that someday I wanted to come to his. But he had to be a big boy and finish school first, and then some day he'd have his own office just like me.

I could feel it working; I was on to something.

I re-tucked his little blue Catholic school shirt into his pants to meet dress code, straightened his tie and belt, and walked him to the front door.

The two ladies, who had been watching the entire time, ducked out of sight as we approached the door. He had no idea that they'd been watching. In the door he went, and up the stairs to his class – just in time for the school bell.

I walked back to my car holding my breath, completely drained for the third day in a row. I now had to go start my day at work.

Just as my hand hit the car door, I heard one of the ladies call out my name. "Jim!"

My heart sank as I imagined him upstairs crying in the classroom.

I turned around and saw the two ladies trotting toward me, big smiles.

"You look like you need a hug. We were watching the whole time, but didn't know what to do. You are such a good dad. He's upstairs and he's fine."

That one singular moment and that gigantic hug made up for all the shit I had ever gotten as a SGD. A little Catholic school principal, well over sixty-five years old, and her stern school administrator, taller than me, gave me a hug and said that I was a good dad. It was all I needed to get through the rest of the school year, and every year after that.

I wish I could thank them today.

Then one year it finally happened: he got onto the school bus on the first day of school with no looking back. It was like the first time he ever slept through the night into the morning. It just happened. He had grown up over-night and overcame an obstacle. It was never an issue again. And he certainly wasn't upset when I dropped him off for college, I can tell you that.

I'd never felt so proud.

That same school administrator was at the door on 9/11/01 when I zoomed up to the school after the attacks on New York. We were all terrified for what else would unfold during the day, and I wanted the kids home. She had them ready and waiting for me. I'm sure there were many parents who did the same.

Now you might be wondering what a gay dad like me was doing in a place like a Catholic school. I know it makes no sense.

It was one of those issues where I couldn't fight with their mom. I tried a little bit, but I just felt that if I had pushed it she would push back too. I was irrationally fearful those days, feeling like I didn't have the support I would need to truly fight it. Today, it would never happen this way and I would fight hard. Back then, I didn't feel like I had a choice.

I don't remember all of the details, but I checked my journal and there sat the entry from the day she told me she had enrolled the kids in Catholic school.

Maybe I should have fought harder. But I was scared. Her involvement in the Church was getting deeper and deeper, including frequent weekend re-treats that we managed our schedules around. While I certainly supported her initiatives, I also didn't know what it could eventually mean for us.

Coward?

My daughter had been in public school for a couple of years, and was do-ing just fine. My son was in his last year of Pre-K, the same one that his sister went to, and was on track to go to the same public school as well.

The day she told me, I had just dropped my son off at his nursery school on a beautiful spring morning, one of those where the trees have just gotten to full bloom and the sky is as bright as it can be.

I was checking my voicemail, and sure enough, there was a message from their mother saying that she was enrolling the kids in Catholic school.

I was pulling into the parking lot of my agency and decided I better call her back. This was before text messaging, so you actually had to call and talk to people!

I left the car running while we talked.

Their mom went on to tell me that she decided to enroll the kids in Catho-lic school because it would be good for them; it was a safe environment.

Good for them, or good for her? I thought to myself.

Evidently the enrollment period was ending soon, so she took the liberty of filling out the paperwork and getting them two slots.

I know I don't have to justify my commitment to my children, but c'mon, this didn't seem right at all. I did everything for those kids every year…physi-cals, immunizations, shopping for clothing, organizing school supplies – you name it; I did it all. In fact I felt like it was all on me. Suddenly, she decides to enroll them in Catholic school, and I don't get a vote?!?

What's the agenda here? I could feel a Catholic agenda brewing for a while now. I could see where it was going. I feared where it was going.

Again, I have nothing against the Catholic Church. Nothing. But I was worried they'd have something against me.

Now mind you, she knew how I felt about public education. I am a huge proponent. I don't believe in segregation of any kind, religion included. We had talked about it several times. I had even been working on the Tylenol Scholarship Fund at my agency for the last few years.

She also knew how I felt about the Catholic religion. I am not a personal proponent. I don't believe in organized religion or all the dogma that comes along with it. That doesn't mean I'm not spiritual; my beliefs are on my own terms. Everyone is entitled to their own beliefs, and I respected hers. I expected the same respect in return.

She acknowledged that she knew I'd be uncomfortable, but that she had already enrolled them. The decision was made and the paperwork was done.

I voiced my opinion, and she pushed back. Hard.

It was one of those moments that I had to trust my gut. Everyone I told later said that I was crazy to agree to it, but I had to trust my gut. How could a gay father allow his children to go to a Catholic school, when the Catholic religion is filled with hatred toward gay people?

"I know," I would say in response.

Eyes wide open; the bigger picture here was keeping my kids.

"Agree to agree." I ate my own words.

She had so much more on her side than I did at that time, despite the fact that we had joint physical custody, joint legal custody, and that I was paying much more in child support than required by law.

"Take money out of the equation."

"Document every night you're with the kids."

I kept hearing my lawyer over and over in my head.

While I may have thought I was in the right, I did not have the court of popular opinion on my side in any manner.

Judges sided with the mom in most cases, religion was publically and defiantly anti-gay, and she had a community of people backing up her every move.

I had Christopher and I had my lawyer. Christopher said he would support whatever my decision; my lawyer said to cave. I caved.

I went into it figuring that if there were ever a problem then I would make a stink about it then. The truth is, there never was a problem. The kids were embraced at that school, and they did fine. The school principal and administrator are certainly proof of that.

That same principal went on to publically say that the Joseph family was a model family, and that the school would be a better place if every family were like the Josephs. Wow. This was long before the Pope said that it was acceptable for gay people to be members of the Church.

I was very sad to see that principal eventually retire; she had become such a fixture. Then the school administrator also moved to another town when her husband got a transfer at work. I felt like my supporters were leaving me, but that was okay. They were there when I really needed them the first few years.

Did I do the right thing? Did I make the right decision? Did I fight hard enough? Should I have caved so easily? I took one for the team and it seems to have worked out in the long run.

Here I am a gay father in a Catholic school!

Deep breaths.

While I didn't fit in at all, not by a long shot, no one was ever rude to me. Not to my face anyway, which is all I cared about.

I got to know the parents through the years, but other than a few exceptions, nothing was really meaningful. The parents always cozied up with the kids' mom, and politely smiled to me out of obligation. Her bond with them was more automatic; I was just a dad standing in the corner most of the time.

Catholic bonds run deep, so I put up a wall of protection around me. I felt like I had to put up a wall, so maybe it was my doing.

I'd sit mostly alone at school events; feeling more isolated than I think anyone should bear. But I was there for my kids, and they were better off for having me there, so I attended and sat quietly. I didn't need to make friends, I just needed to support my kids and make them feel comfortable. That was the priority.

I did lunch duty every semester, attended teacher conferences, chaperoned class field trips, and cheered at my kids' games. I tried to be around that school as much as I could, so at least no one could say that I was hiding.

There is one blessing of a Catholic school, I will say: school uniforms. They are amazing. No hard choices in the morning, no shopping sprees for designer labels, and they certainly wash well over and over again. While I'm definitely not one for being a cookie cutter, I do love school uniforms.

The process of sizing and buying the uniforms took us awhile to master. If you don't hit it right, then you're dealing with long lines and backorders. We had a few years of jerry-rigged pants, stretched tights, and pinned skirts to hold us over until a shipment came in. After a few taxing attempts, though, we were pros at sustaining the uniforms year after year and supplementing our inventory as the kids grew.

Ok, so there was one other thing I liked about that school too – the talent show.

The one shining moment in the school every year was the annual talent show. On the surface, it was dreadful. There wasn't a lick of talent to be seen anywhere. Under my breath, I would call it the "no talent show."

Sure, there was singing, dancing, and music…if that's what you want to call it. But it was brutal. I think the numerous acts of attempted Irish dancing almost killed me each year.

Don't get me wrong, it's not like my kids were superstars by any means either. One year at a piano recital, my son was supposed to perform *Twinkle Twinkle Little Star*. He was wearing a little shirt and tie, holding his sheet music. When he got to the piano, he plucked away at the first verse and then stopped.

Twinkle twinkle little star
How I wonder what you are

He picked up his sheet music, bowed to the audience, and walked off the stage. That was the extent of his solo performance career. That was it!

My daughter didn't find her voice until much later in grammar school. For each talent show, she would do group skits but nothing solo. Once she started performing on her own though, she trained her voice into a beautiful instrument in high school. I doubt she'll ever quit her day job to perform, but it's wonderful that she has a talent that she can use on her own terms.

But for three years in a row at the grammar school talent show, there was an awesome glimmer of light.

Out of nowhere, this one little boy started singing disco songs as his solo performance. He finally put the "talent" in the talent show.

I missed the first year when he sang *I Will Survive*, but the kids told me that he brought the house down. I was bummed that I missed it, although I definitely didn't miss the rest of the show.

The second year he sang *Knock On Wood*, and I was in awe.

Now admittedly, it may have been the immense talent gap that made him stand out, or his choice of music, but it was love at first sight.

The kids had been telling me, "Wait until you hear him sing. You're going to love him. I can't wait for you to hear him sing, Dad."

I had been dozing in and out during the show, but I woke up when I recognized the opening bars of the song.

He was beyond good. Shouts of support came all during his performance, as did a standing ovation at the end.

While many were saluting his talent, I was saluting his bravery. A little boy singing disco songs at a Catholic school talent show. Bravo!

I walked into the school office one day to drop off paperwork, and there on the bulletin board was a picture of this kid backstage with Donna Summer. I felt jealous! But what made me most proud was how the school embraced him. He became of symbol of joy to that school, and everyone loved him.

There was another little boy that we knew in town who became known for singing show tunes at school, at the pool, and wherever else he would go. His mom would ask me what to do about it and my reply was simply, "Sing along with him and take him to shows in New York."

So while none of us would ever be famous on Broadway, there was one thing that we did become famous for through the years: our school lunches, as made by Christopher. Our lunches became legendary; as did the little notes and stickers we left on the bags. As the kids got older, we had to temper our enthusiasm, however, because my daughter told us that the other boys were making fun of my son. Isn't that sad? Growing up can suck sometimes.

Oh no, I'd be remiss to leave out Special Person Day – the one day each year that students brought a "special person" to school for lunch. My daughter took me one year, as did my son another year. My father went one year, as did their grandmother on their mom's side.

The year that my son asked Christopher to go, panic set in. "He wants to take me," was Christopher's response to me, with terror in his voice. "What will people say?"

The truth is that anything that could be said would have already been said at this point, so what could anyone possibly add in now? I encouraged him to go and support our son. He was nervous, but he got through it, mostly because the principal spent the entire lunch sitting next to Christopher, sending a not-so-subtle signal to the other parents. It was very generous of her, once again.

The big juggling act came when the kids would get sick. This is every working parent's dilemma. Back then, before there was technology in place to help us work from home, their sick day was my sick day. Whenever they would get a runny nose, it was like a contest to see how sick they really were. Should I push them to school anyway? Should I just bring them to work? Should I stay home with them?

My diagnoses were always an imperfect science, and it became a negotiating act with the kids. One year my son was convinced that he had swine flu, and I was convinced that he was making a mountain out of a molehill. Turned out he was right! Other times I'd keep them home only to discover that they were totally fine by 10:30am. It was a crapshoot at best.

I even put a couch in my office at the agency so that the kids could hang out there on their days off or when they weren't feeling well. All they really needed was a comfortable couch, a warm blanket, lots of liquids, and they would be fine. I could give them that at work or at home; I think they loved the attention they got at work. My son especially loved coming to the office with me.

I always worried that he would say he was sick just so he could hang out on my couch at work and play video games. You have to be part detective, part nurse, and part debate champion to be a good parent.

As I changed jobs through the years, even going into New York, my son would come spend time with me at work, as did my daughter. In fact, as my daughter got older, she would come into the city and go explore while I was in the office. While it was difficult for me to let her go out in the city on her own, I also knew that she was growing up. She was getting ready to explore on her own, and has been exploring the world ever since!

While they never wanted to believe my medical diagnosis, I also didn't believe them either. Mutual skepticism I suppose.

One year, my daughter convinced herself that she couldn't see well enough anymore. I was highly doubtful, I'm not sure why, but I just had an intuition that she was making it up so that she could get glasses.

The girl gets what she wants; let me assure you of that. She faked her way through the eye exam and convinced the optometrist that she needed glasses. The prescription was a light one, and sure enough, even the doctor said that he kind of gave into her. I bet she still has those glasses today.

While Christopher was the resident cook, he also turned out to be the resident doctor as well. Sure, I did all the appointments, but he was a master of at-home remedies and diagnosis. He was much more equipped than me, and they seemed to believe whatever he told them.

They'd show him every scrape and bump, and he'd fix it. I guess they thought of me as the guy would couldn't cook or put on a Band-Aid, which I was fine with. He also made a much bigger deal out of it than I ever did. I remained calm and didn't let anything sway me; I think they were looking for a little drama and attention, and he gave it to them in spades.

No problem for me. I thought it was adorable.

Of course, no one at school saw all of this. They only saw an ex-husband who turned gay, living with his handsome boyfriend, with his poor ex-wife at home with two young kids. The difference between perception and reality was mind-boggling, to the point where I really had a hard time handling it. But I had no way to really change the perception. In the end I didn't care, because all I really wanted was to be a dad and try to give the kids the proper home they needed. I didn't really care what other families thought; I knew who I was and I knew what we had created for them.

If it meant we had to make some tough choices for our lives, then so be it...

CHAPTER 13

I Did What I Had To Do

I know it's probably hard to believe, but I've never been too crazy about Father's Day.

With two adult men in the house taking care of the children, I never felt comfortable being singled out on this one day, even though I am the dad. While the day was meant for me, I guess I always wanted to share it with Christopher.

Christopher did just as much for the kids as I did, even more in some cases. He was basically a stepfather, but we never spoke about it that way. I wish I had done more to acknowledge him on Father's Day too, but Christopher was still just Christopher like on any other day.

Admittedly, Father's Day got off to a bad start with me right from the beginning.

My very first Father's Day, with my daughter less than a year old, was a non-event. I had left Johnson & Johnson and was working at Arm & Hammer. We had just launched the new Fridge-Freezer Pack of Arm & Hammer Baking Soda, the first product innovation for that brand in decades, and we were now working on the launch of a brand new toothpaste that contained both baking soda and peroxide. It was the first of its kind, called PeroxiCare.

We were holding regional meetings with the sales team and they were starting on Monday, the day after Father's Day. My boss asked me to leave on Sunday so that we could all have dinner together ahead of the meeting. It was completely unnecessary as far as I could tell, especially given the holiday and especially given the fact that the sales team wasn't arriving until the next afternoon.

"But it's Father's Day," I said to him (he was also a father). "Can't we just leave Monday morning? It's my first Father's Day. If we leave Monday morning, we will still get to the meeting in plenty of time." I stated my case as a brand new dad.

"A day away from home is Father's Day to me," he replied. So I packed up my bags and missed my very first Father's Day with my daughter. That didn't happen again, let me tell you. I took it as a signal that I had to get my priorities straight.

While I was doing very well at work, I was starting to feel like success could come at a sacrifice to my family. My new baby was the priority, and given my role at home, I had to be around. I wanted to be around.

I also figured that there were many ways to tackle my career – lots of ways to skin the marketing cat. I could find a better way to be successful at work, without having to be away from my family so much.

Truthfully, my family needed me as their dad more than any company needed me as their marketer. That first Father's Day made me realize that I had some very tough choices ahead of me.

To look at me today, running a huge agency, you wouldn't know that I managed my career around raising my kids. When they were young and needed me, I was home. I made the choice to be home; I made the choice to make the kids a priority. I did what I needed to do.

I left Arm & Hammer soon after that first Father's Day, and jumped off the big corporate ladder by joining a small, independently-owned agency in Connecticut – I came on board to open up a local office to serve Pennsylvania and New Jersey.

It was the best decision I ever made, because it allowed me to work from home and be there with the kids. It gave me the kind of flexibility I needed to take good care of them; it gave me the kind of flexibility that they needed from me.

Looking back, I'm not sure I had a choice. I did what I had to do.

With this new job working from home, I could get them up in the morning, get them ready for their day, and then be there at night for dinner, baths, and bedtime. I could also run out during the day for whatever they needed. When they were super young, I didn't travel that much, so I was there most of the time.

Keep in mind that this was long before WFH – Working From Home – was such a social phenomenon. There were no cell phones, no Wi-Fi, no Internet. We didn't even have email yet. Working from home was not common, so it really was a step off of the marketing career path for me. It was a step off of a corporate ladder, where I had been excelling.

It was 1994, and we were still reeling from the first bombing of the World Trade Center in New York. I was prioritizing my life and making decisions to make it work for us.

As the kids started going to school and started becoming more independent themselves, then I made career decisions that allowed me to progress too. I advanced as they advanced.

As the kids started to settle in, I moved the agency out of the house and built up my team to handle all the new business I had won. I didn't need to be around the house during the day as much so I moved out into a proper office with an expanded team. The little agency was booming and I had to drive its growth.

Success begets success, and it was time to advance it forward.

As the kids started to get busy with their own school activities, I left that small agency and started my own firm. I figured that there was no reason I couldn't do the agency thing myself, so why work for someone else? I was ready for the next move because the kids were ready for the next move.

That was right around the time I met Christopher.

Our biggest client was Tylenol, but we soon started expanding our base beyond my alma mater Johnson & Johnson. We actually created content for the very first website for Tylenol, but we also built the first interactive website for Congoleum flooring, where customers could send in pictures of their home and see what it would look like with all new flooring. Sounds like nothing now, but at the time this technology was innovative. This was way before social media.

Christopher made some hard choices as well. When we first moved in together, he was working over an hour and a half away in another state. The commute was hell, as were his hours. He quit that job and joined me at the agency so that we could focus our efforts on making it a success. He stayed at the office all day and ran the operations so that I could be out with clients. It was a match that worked perfectly and the business thrived, as did our home life.

People asked me all the time how we could live and work together as "partners" and "partners." It's easy when you're with a terrific person who motivates you at work and at home! How ironic that the name of the agency was CP Partners.

When I knew that the kids could handle me being away a bit more, I sold the agency to advance my career. I didn't sell for the money; I sold to get a bigger job at a bigger agency. It was a good deal because it made me the President of what was then the largest marketing services agency in New York: Arc. It was part of the Leo Burnett agency based in Chicago.

I commuted back and forth to New York because I had Christopher near our house. He could help with the kids when I was tied up with work.

Here I was back in a big corporation, but I was ready for it. There were layers of management and multiple project teams to navigate and coordinate. I was prepared because I had the support I needed at home.

We were working on every new model year Cadillac and it was exciting.

Soon after we sold the agency, Christopher left his position to stay at home to take care of the house and the kids. He became a stay-at-home father, although not by name. My hours got longer and I started traveling more and more, so we needed someone to keep home base, much like I maintained home base when the kids were babies and toddlers. I was creating cereal promotions for Kellogg's, and he was serving it at home.

With a parent company in Chicago, I had to go there several times a month, plus now my clients were located all over the country. I couldn't be home every single night and we needed someone to hold down the fort and be available 24/7.

This was no small thing: Christopher gave up his career to stay at home for me and for the kids. This just didn't happen back then. This was long before the #SAHD (Stay At Home Dad).

Christopher took over all of the domestic duties. I focused on work, while he focused on home. While the kids were still the priority, they were getting busier and busier and didn't need me to be quite so attentive. The countdown to college tuition was starting, so I had to get a move on. Christopher made tough choices so that I could make tough choices, too.

A few years later, as the company started moving resources to the headquarters in Chicago, I started feeling the pressure to go to Chicago too. While it was never stated, there was an underlying sense that things would be changing. So I jumped ship to make sure I could keep my family intact on the east coast.

I did what I had to do; I had to jump ship to make sure I could be around for the kids. I couldn't move them to Chicago. I probably could have made a commuting arrangement work, but that would mean that I wouldn't see them during the week and I wasn't going to live that way.

So I went to yet another small, independent organization that promised great entrepreneurial rewards along with a schedule that I could arrange around the kids. After one year, that didn't pan out, so I contacted some former colleagues and went back to running a large agency within the same company that had bought CP Partners. I had relationships with some of the senior managers there, so it was a no-brainer to join them.

When I joined the agency, it was called Saatchi & Saatchi Consumer Healthcare, but then I dramatically reinvented it to go after a broader client portfolio with expanded capabilities. I renamed it Saatchi & Saatchi Wellness.

I made the most of my time there, winning numerous awards, including Agency of the Year, Most Creative Agency, and a Grand Clio for our Ambien CR "Rooster" campaign.

It was arguably one of the best assignments of my career, having the perfect mix of being challenging, rewarding, and independent. I made some incredible friendships there that have stood the test of time.

In fact, I still have many friends from every stage of my career; they've all become a big part of who I am.

I started my first marketing blog while working at Saatchi & Saatchi Wellness, and was floored when people actually read and commented on my posts.

You mean people want to pay attention to what I have to say?!

My role at Saatchi & Saatchi Wellness, including navigating its reinvention, was an amazing experience that could have lasted a lifetime, but I had much more aggressive goals. I hit the glass ceiling in that job, so I left.

I moved on to a new entrepreneurial opportunity from there but it didn't pan out either, unfortunately. I was hoping for a much more aggressive arrangement to yield much more aggressive results. When it became clear that wasn't going to be the case, I exited for what turned out to be a much bigger opportunity.

If at first you don't succeed, try try try again.

It was during this time that I started writing professional marketing books. I created a trilogy of books that show how to market brands and build experiences for customers, called *The Experience Effect*.

My books were aimed at all types of companies: big brands, small brands, and personal brands. Those books helped me find my voice on branding and gave me a platform to increase my industry presence.

I was finally ready to put myself out there professionally and offer my point of view, after years in the making.

I was recruited to my current agency, a global communications firm called Cohn & Wolfe. After my first year there, we won Agency of the Year! Just this year we won Consumer Launch of the Year for one of my biggest clients at Microsoft. We've also won back-to-back awards for being a "best place to work." Regardless of the awards, I'm so honored to be there.

I've never worked so hard at work in my life, and I'm in my fifties!

It's a big job and it requires a lot of late nights and a lot of travel. But the kids were in high school when I started and now they're in college so there's no problem with me putting in that kind of time. Christopher is still home to take care of us all, whenever we need anything.

I also became a professor at NYU. The Dean first asked me to create a weekend intensive class based on my first book. Of course I jumped at the chance. I've always wanted to teach, and always felt that if it weren't for marketing, I'd be teaching. Now I do both.

I learn as much from the students as they do from me, if not more. I've since gone on to teach graduate level classes in Integrated Marketing each semester. I like to think that I'm helping shape the next generation of talent in the marketing industry, which makes me feel like I'm doing something important. Perhaps this is just another aspect of my paternal instincts.

I'm asked all the time how I do it, and how I keep it all going.

Christopher, that's how.

He motivates and supports me every step of the way. As do the kids, in their own way.

In many ways, though, I am making up for lost time.

These are career moves that I probably should have made in my thirties, rather than my forties and beyond. There have been colleagues that have criticized my job changes through the years, but I shrug them off. While all of you were chasing promotions and career advancements all those years, I was changing diapers and attending teacher conferences. I didn't question your career choices then so don't question mine now.

I put my family first back then.

JOURNAL: 5/28/01
The kids don't have school on Thurs and Friday b4 Mem Day
w/e, so I took those days off to spend with them. So this week,
they spent Mon night, Wed night, and then all the way thru to
the next Tuesday morning. Here's what we did:
zoo
Trenton Thunder game
played baseball
movies
bowling
picnic at (friend's) house
It was a great holiday w/e. We also spent time getting clothes
ready for summer, etc.

It's not an easy thing to explain on the job front. It wasn't acceptable for a man to make these kinds of career choices. There must have been something wrong?!?

I have to get aggressive now with my career to make the advances everyone else was getting when we were all younger. I still have career aspirations; I'm not done yet! It's this dad's turn now…it's a different kind of Father's Day.

Now I'm publishing blog posts every day, writing for *Entrepreneur* magazine and *Huffington Post*. I'm enjoying every minute of it, despite the out-of-control pace and the mental fatigue that sets in every Friday right around 2:30pm. I could never have done any of this when the kids were young. I wouldn't have even tried.

Anyone looking to take that away from me with snipes about jumping jobs can shove it.

I was recently at a ceremony where I was inducted into a Marketing Hall of Fame, a huge honor. Someone at my dinner table announced to everyone, "Every time I see Jim he has a different job!" Gee, thanks.

I did what I had to do.

I am happy I made the decisions I did in those years because they made us who we all are now. The kids are happy and healthy, and advancing in their own lives. Christopher is about to embark on doing something he really wants to do, now that he's not needed at home quite so much.

We've also made tough choices about where to live over the years as well.

There was no way that I could leave Bucks County, PA; I had to stay close to where their mom lived so both of us could be with the kids.

We did what we could do with our homes, as we could afford it. We grew our house as the kids, their needs, and our need for privacy grew.

For our first home, we chose what we knew and were comfortable with: New Hope.

We chose New Hope because we felt safe there, not only because we were gay but because we had kids too. I'm sorry to say that there weren't a lot of towns back then that would accept a kid with a gay father.

With so many other gay people in town, we figured we'd be more accepted there as a gay couple with children. We figured the children would be more accepted there too.

We felt like it was our best option, and that turned out to be true. Plus it was still only twenty minutes from their mom's house; shuffling back and forth wouldn't be that hard.

We loved living in New Hope, partly because we lived right on the river and could walk into town along the canal. We'd walk into town for ice cream, rollerblade into town for dinner, and climb all around the rocks along the riverbank. We all loved going into the river to skip stones, and brave the rapids. We couldn't get enough of it.

But there was something even better about New Hope, a little bonus that few people knew about – the LGD.

Local Gay Discount.

There were no hashtags back then, just an unspoken gift that the local business people would do for the local gay people…a twenty percent discount off the retail price. I guess it was their way of sending a "wink" whenever we bought something in the community. It was a little benefit to balance all the other crap we had to put up with. I never got sick of that!

Three floods later, however, we got a little sick of living on the river. It was time to move.

When the kids started to enter high school we picked a small town away from the river called Newtown. It was closer to their school and closer to their friends – their social life was starting to form and we had to make it easier on them. Newtown wasn't exactly gay-friendly, but it was right for the kids now that they were older. We didn't love it there, but it completely worked for them and they were the priority.

It was also a much bigger house for each of the kids to have their own individual space. These are choices you make as a family.

It's funny but no matter what house we lived in and no matter what the layout, I swear that I could still hear the kids breathing at night. I would lie in bed and focus on their breathing, making sure that they were settled into bed. If they were sick with colds, then my listening became even more acute.

When they would talk in their sleep, I could hear every word no matter how soundly I was sleeping. And when my son would sleepwalk as a youngster, I would always guide him right back to his bed without stirring him awake.

I look at gay fathers today with such respect and a little bit of envy. In many ways we would have loved being the sole parents, raising our kids just by ourselves. We could have lived life more on our terms, doing what we knew to be right for them without any added pressure or demands.

I am sure we would have moved to New York to avoid the horrendous commute I've endured year after year, and to be closer to the friends we had made. I've had a two-hour plus commute each way for years. Sure, we've tried tiny apartments in New York on and off again to help manage life, but home has always been with the kids.

We would have had much deeper relationships with other parents more like us, and would have been able to share some of our experiences and probably handled things better. It's been almost impossible to add friendships to the schedule we've lived all these years.

But that was not our journey, and that is not our story. So be it. I wouldn't change the kids or our lives now for the world.

We made the choices we needed to make, at the time we needed to make them, to make it all work. None of them were sacrifices; they were tangible and thoughtful choices to do what was right for the family.

I did what I had to do. I would do it again if faced with the same challenges. No regrets, just lessons learned.

I also did what I needed to do to keep the peace…

CHAPTER 14
Mother's Day

I've always made a very concerted effort to get along with the kids' mom. Like I said, we agreed to agree most of the time, which I truly appreciate, even now.

I am sure there were many times that she didn't agree with me, questioned my decisions, and disliked me living with a man. Aside from some occasional drama, she didn't show it. I have to give her credit for that.

While this is a story about my journey, her choices certainly impacted my life with the kids. In the beginning, most of her free time was spent dating and socializing, just like mine was. I would even run into her at the Cartwheel!

Over time though, I felt like her relationship with the Church came out of nowhere, at least to me, and had a sudden, profound effect on the children's lives. Her involvement in the Church made me very uncomfortable and at times made me worry that any control I may have had over our lives could be taken away from me.

I worried a lot those days.

On the one hand it was none of my business, yet I was impacted by it. I wanted it to be none of my business, but I couldn't turn a blind eye to it either.

She had her priorities and I had mine.

I actually liked it better when she was dating all of the time. At least she was out socially and would leave the kids with me. I could handle that; what I couldn't anticipate was the direction that the Catholic Church might take her and the kids.

I put my head down and plowed ahead.

My priority was getting the kids through each day, through each school year, and through each rite of passage: from the first period to the first love to the first driving lesson. I was there from colds to allergies and from braces to vaccinations. One day at a time!

My favorite of them all was chicken pox.

Both kids contracted chicken pox at the exact same time, but because they were so young it was pretty mild: no high fever, no massive itching, no scarring at all. But we did have lots of oatmeal baths!

The best part?

I took time off from work to stay in the apartment with them; we were in our pajamas for days! I didn't exercise for a week. It was heaven.

I dotted their little bodies and faces with pink calamine lotion; they were adorable. They were very contagious, but felt fine, so they were filled with energy. It was a vacation at home with Dad! We played games (including Candy Land), ordered pizza, and watched Disney movies all day long.

My daughter had been a big fan of *The Sound of Music* ever since she was a little kid. We must have played that movie six times that week, and she sang and danced to every single song. She knew every single word, even at that age!

I completely disconnected from work that week; they had me all to themselves.

Trust me, I'm not trying to paint myself as the perfect dad by any means. I was horrible when I was teaching the kids how to drive and I was even worse helping them with school projects. In fact I failed miserably in the dad department in these areas.

I have a very bad combination of absolute perfectionism and unrelenting impatience when it comes to those awful school projects. I would pay money just to have someone else do them for us.

Enter Christopher!

He makes the best damn Squanto village I have ever seen. There's no solar system better on the planet than one painted with Christopher's vision. He's a master at using dry ice to create just the right effect. There was never a more creative poster done by a fourth grader. Ever.

He seems to have muscle memory when it comes to these things. When the same project repeats again for the next kid, he puts a different spin on it and figures out how to do it even better.

Great – I'll just sit at the table here and do some work.

Of course, I was the one in charge of actually getting these projects to school the next day in one piece; no small feat, I will have you know. Talk about pressure! We would have these fragile projects double protected in bubble wrap, boxed, padded, and gingerly placed in the car. You'd have thought they were made of gold. As far as I was concerned, they were made of gold.

The greatest challenge, though, bar none, was Mother's Day.

For some reason, maybe a combination of guilt and wanting harmony, we hosted Mother's Day more than a few times over the years.

Sometimes we had their mom with us, sometimes she was traveling and we'd have the kids alone, and sometimes their mom would bring an added guest with her to our house. We never knew what we'd be getting into, but we were happy to host, at least the first few times. The kids were always excited when their mom was coming over. I guess it was a glimpse of being normal.

There was nothing normal about it, but then again, what is "normal?"

To get ready for the kids' Mother's Day celebration, we would plan, grocery shop, decorate, and cook. Correction – there was no "we;" Christopher did the heavy lifting. I helped prep, set the table, and did the cleanup while Christopher handled all the rest. The kids were of course just being little kids.

Now mind you, this wasn't for our mothers at all. In fact, my mother was always at her home in Virginia. This was for the kids' mom. Correction – this was for the kids.

I'm not sure if we were crazy or just gluttons for punishment. Trust me, it wasn't a lot of fun, but we did what we had to do.

One year's surprise guest was one of their mom's boyfriends. Oh, boy!

While we were preparing all the food, we invited the mom and the boyfriend to go sit out on the balcony overlooking the river. The view was amazing, and we were trying to be good hosts.

One thing led to another, and there she as sitting on his lap in the midst of a massive make-out session, with the two kids looking at them through the glass door. It was like they were at the zoo, watching animals in a cage. Their mom was oblivious, and I didn't even know because I was downstairs helping

Christopher get dinner ready.

Christopher's mom happened to be with us for Mother's Day that year and she's the one who had the "room with the view," shall we say. When she saw the kids watching and they started asking her questions, she quickly gathered them up and brought them downstairs to their room. It was the fastest ticket to a marathon game of Candy Land I have ever seen. Queen Frostine to the rescue.

The next year we had their mom's mother and her grandmother over for Mother's Day. Three generations of mothers. That's the year she spilled her meal all over our white couch. It was time to replace it, especially since the chicken fat left a permanent stain. Yes, a permanent stain.

Was I keeping up appearances? Yes. Was I appeasing the kids? Definitely. Was I managing the situation? Every single day.

The best Mother's Days were actually the years she was traveling out of the country, and there were several, including just this last year. I hate to say it this way, but it's true. It was glorious when she would travel to one of her numerous retreats, spiritual voyages, or just vacations, because we didn't have to deal with her schedule. We could just live and be ourselves. I hate to say it this way, but it's true.

One of those years she was traveling, we had Christopher's mom in town again for Mother's Day. Feeling guilty that the kids weren't with their mom that day, we went overboard and planned out an entire picnic brunch. This was no typical picnic mind you. We are talking crab cakes, ham croissant sandwiches, and pigs in a blanket.

Oh, and some Pepperidge Farm goldfish.

We decided to take a walk along the river to the State Park on the canal that wasn't too far away; it was a perfect location for our picnic. The kids wanted to ride their new bikes, even though they were not completely adept at riding them quite yet.

I kept reminding my son to stay by my side. But he was being a little boy and couldn't help but want to go a lot faster than I could walk. When he would get really far ahead, I would yell up to him to stop. It was a constant battle for the entire mile.

He started to get farther and farther ahead and pretended like he couldn't hear me anymore. It's not like it really mattered; he was perfectly safe. There was no one else around. I was just worried that he would ride right into the canal. He was in no worse a danger than a whole lot of canal mud. I should have just relaxed.

But sure enough, I saw him slowly edging toward the canal. I started screaming, dropped the baskets of food to the ground, and ran up to him just in time to grab his ankles before he and his bike went into mud. Laundry disaster averted.

All in a day, Mother's Day that is.

Now at the time, friends thought I was crazy to host the mom so much. While it would probably never need to happen today, at the time I was just trying to keep the peace. We were the consummate hosts, regardless of how we felt about it.

I never said a word when she used all of the child support money on herself and her house. I still bought virtually all of the kids' clothes and paid for all of their healthcare costs. I bought sports equipment and paid for all of their registration fees for school activities. I started college funds that I managed and contributed to on a monthly basis. I paid for virtually everything.

I'm not complaining – I guess in some ways I'm still trying to protect myself, even now. It's sad that I still feel the need to document everything.

Truthfully, I liked being in control and the money allowed me to do that. First of all, I am their dad so it's my responsibility. Second of all, controlling the money meant keeping her at bay. She couldn't really afford to suddenly have a problem with me being gay. I considered the money I gave to her each month and everything that I shelled out in between as basic insurance. It was my life insurance, to keep my life moving forward.

Could you accuse me of being manipulative? Yep, guilty as charged.

Could you accuse me of managing all of our emotions? Twice convicted.

Could you blame me? Maybe, but it worked.

I never said a word when friends would complain about her to me, commenting that she didn't watch the children closely enough. I just paid a little closer attention to make up for it.

I also didn't say a word when I found out she was taking the kids to Church every morning before school, at something like 7:00am. While I didn't understand the necessity, the kids didn't seem to object that much, so I let it go. I wouldn't have been able to win that fight.

I'll never know if I should have fought harder.

I did say no when she asked me to take the kids to Church on the Sundays they were with me; my lawyer said that I had no obligation when they were with me. When they were old enough to ask me themselves, then I drove them back and forth to Church at *their* discretion. Every time they asked.

Today I would certainly say a lot more on the subject because I would have the law on my side. But back then, one small fight could have led to a much bigger battle that I wasn't prepared to perhaps lose. I pushed it as far as I was comfortable, even though I had joint custody.

The problem is that at the time, any fictional account she could have written about me would have been considered more believable than any amount of truth from me. While I had my journal, she had a community of support. She had an entire social culture of support. Remember, this was twenty years ago and times were very different legally and socially.

I also didn't say a word when she publicly "outed" me in print (before I was ready) in a Christian newspaper, shaping the story to put herself in the limelight. I found out from an employee at my agency who was afraid we'd lose clients as a result. To be fair, even I was afraid we'd lose clients. This was way before my Tylenol ad was "out."

I just put it in my journal and went back to the conference room in the sky in downtown Philadelphia to meet with my lawyer again. She said to keep calm; confronting her could possibly lead to a legal battle, which could be risky at best. "Don't rattle the cage," was the advice she gave. It was good advice, given the times.

So I carried on in silence, focused on caring for the kids and getting us all through it.

"Just hang on until they're eighteen," is what I kept saying to myself. Until they're eighteen. Eighteen

> JOURNAL: *January*
> *Kids were sick on and off for a few weeks. (She) did nothing to*
> *help them feel better, make them not get sicker, etc. She sent*

them to school with fevers, rarely gave them medicine, and basically took no time out of her busy schedule to make them better. Very sad for them, frustrating for me.

Did 2 school projects with (my daughter) on the weekends: solar system and Squanto.

Was a guest reader on Thurs 1/18 in (my son's) class and handed out little presents for his classmates.

Jan 25 Thurs – (My son's) teacher conference at 4:30

No matter what I did, she still had society on her side. It seemed as if she could do whatever she wanted.

And while I didn't have that luxury, I incorrectly assumed that a few people would defend me when needed…

CHAPTER 15
Bulletproof Vest

I have to say that I got quite good at anticipating problems. I could easily outsmart the "frenemies" and I got to know their game. I found ways to head them off at the pass, most of the time anyway. I developed a survival instinct that kept me on my toes, made me prepared at every corner, and worked well to preserve my career and my family.

I sound so paranoid – welcome to life as a dad. I just couldn't trust "them." But I was not going to get caught off guard.

It happened a few times, I have to admit. It was the ones I had kept close by my side and the ones that I trusted the most that took me by surprise. It took me awhile to realize that they could cause us harm, too.

While I thought I knew who to watch out for, it was the posers that got me every time.

First we have the gay men who we thought were friends but who really wanted to see Christopher and I split up.

I'm not sure if it was jealousy or sport, but there were a lot of guys we met along the way who didn't want to be friends with us as a couple, so they tried to separate us. They'd become friends with one of us, and then work to divide the two of us. Of course it didn't work, mostly because I got pretty expert at sniffing it out.

It happened from day one. Right from the very start there were many gay men that tried to make sure that our relationship didn't get off the ground, including the artist I had dated and who casually introduced me to Christopher

's First Apartment.

First Date with Christopher.

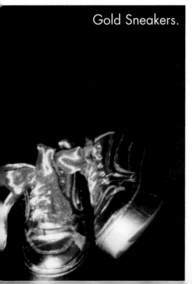
Gold Sneakers.

Boys Night Out.

The Beloved Candy

Which One's Neater?

Which One's N

Making Christmas Cookies.

10th Birthday in Hawaii.

Holiday Card 2010.

Exploring the River.

Salad Bowl of America.

The Best Part of Key West.

Home with Chicken Pox.

Out and About. Dad.

Day of School.

First Day of School.

Good Luck at School.

Work That Dress!

Millennials at
the Millennial.

Eighteen!

e's First Night Home.

Sophie and Her Pack.

A Boy and His Dog.

ie's Favorite Spot.

Saturday Morning Starbucks.

Classic Sophie.

Classic Photo Op Redone.

in the beginning.

I am big into annual holiday parties, so the first year I opened my new agency I wanted to have a holiday party just like when I'd been a part of other organizations. Now that I had my own business, I wanted to start a tradition. Of course, I didn't have any employees to party with, which made it tricky to have a substantial party.

Details.

So I asked Christopher (even though we had just started dating) to join a mutual writer friend that I'd been working with, and we figured we'd ask our artist friend too. Four gay men, who all know each other, seemed to be a fitting first annual holiday party for my agency.

Big mistake.

Not too long into the dinner, Christopher started to act weird. Absent and absent-minded, actually. He basically passed out at the table, and had to go home. The artist offered to bring him home, acting like the big hero, which should have been my first sign.

I didn't hear from Christopher the next day, so of course I started to worry. I called the artist to see what had happened, and got an earful.

The scoop, according to the artist, was that Christopher had a major drinking and drug problem and couldn't hold his own in social situations. The artist went on to say that every time he'd ever been at a party with Christopher, this is exactly what happened. He would lose control because of all the drugs and alcohol he had taken.

He knew this would strike a chord with me because we had talked about how the drug thing and me don't mix, not as a father.

Okay.

Granted, I didn't know Christopher very well yet. I didn't know any of them very well. But it didn't add up. None of us were drinking a lot, and in fact, Christopher was probably drinking less than I was. I really didn't see him leave the table, so I'm not sure when he would have had time to consume that much. His behavior came on very suddenly; a night of partying doesn't produce results that quickly.

It didn't make sense.

When I finally did talk to Christopher, he had no recollection of the night.

None. He asked me what had happened, how he got home, and even if we had even finished dinner.

Of course the artist asked me, "Do you really want that around the kids?" Don't pull the fatherhood argument on me, that is for my use only.

We came to the conclusion that our artist "friend" had laced Christopher's drink, in an effort to embarrass him and to make me question his character.

Sadly, this scenario played out many times through the years where guys would make up rumors to get us to question each other. Granted not always with tampered drinks in the equation, but I'm sure you know what I mean.

It was a game for some of these guys, and it didn't leave much room for making a lot of friends. Then there were friends who were already in relationships but just wanted to fool around; something neither one of us wanted either.

Granted, in some respects this is probably nothing different than what happens in the straight world, but in a small gay community these kinds of things travel fast. Rumors become reality overnight. Like a lot of couples, gay or straight, we had to dodge a lot of bullets to stay together.

Those people are now out of our life.

If that's not enough, then you have the straight friends who just want to have token gay friends, but don't really believe that you're an equal. Oh boy, did we go through a lot of these people. These friends just wanted either a "gay husband" or a "gay best friend" to prove that they were cool. We experienced this with straight men and women, and I'm not sure which was worse.

After a few drinks, however, the truth would always come out. They would slip and talk trash about gay people, forgetting for just a second that the guys sitting in front of them were, in fact, gay. The stereotypes and the slurs would start flying, subtle at first, and then become more and more overt.

We had to make a conscious decision to take these people out of our lives as well. It was hard because in some cases, we had invested a lot of time and emotion into these friendships. We wanted people to accept us as equals – equal friends and equals at parenting as well. So we would overlook a lot at first, until it became so obvious that we couldn't ignore it.

It gets worse.

There were the straight friends who were really closeted gay men who were afraid to face it, but still wanted to have the company of other gay men. They wanted male companionship, or more, but hadn't come to grips with it. These guys were painful, I have to tell you.

I know I should have been more understanding, but it's hard when they were consciously trying to take us down at the same time.

We would constantly ignore all the gay innuendos, and constantly claim ignorance when hit with the question, "Isn't he gay?" Dodging more bullets, but these often came close to the heart.

Everyone just figured we'd be the first to know, which wasn't the case. We didn't care one way or the other; it was their business to work out. But I don't think the wives in those relationships were too thrilled with the attention their husbands tried to get from us. Given my background, I was a threat.

I get it, but I didn't want it.

Meanwhile, we just wanted to have a group of friends who accepted us, gay or straight. These were the friends who proved to be the most dangerous, oddly enough, because it naively took us so long to see through their facades. Then when they didn't get what they wanted, they turned on us.

And they got mean about it.

They would constantly talk with us about how homophobic others were. They constantly reminded me that being gay would hurt my career, and that clients wouldn't want to be around me. They told me that my career would never advance as a result. They would literally point to people and say that despite being nice to my face, these people were stabbing me in the back.

They also constantly reminded Christopher that the kids were my kids, not his, and that he would never have a meaningful relationship with them. They told him that he was facing a life of loneliness because one day I would leave him high and dry, and the kids would never speak to him again.

One woman even told Christopher that I was secretly straight, and that this was just a phase I was going through. She told him that I'd eventually leave him for another woman again, because I prefer women and what I really want is another mother for my children.

As if.

Nice friends, right? Just because they couldn't deal with their own issues, they had to bounce it over to us.

There were times when it got ugly.

We had befriended a single mother in New Hope who was alone with her kids. We did a lot with that family, including spending a lot of alone time with her kids. We wanted to take them in and make them a part of our family.

The mother turned out to be a bit of a problem, shall we say, so we had to creatively work our way out of the relationship. She was causing trouble between our two daughters, roping Christopher into the middle of it. Then he would get mad at the situation, which would create a circle of animosity with the girls that would go back around again to her.

It was a mess. We had enough going on as it was, we certainly didn't need more drama from "friends" so we let that relationship fade away.

The minute the mother figured out that we weren't available anymore, she started slandering Christopher to her daughter, who then told my daughter. She spread rumors about Christopher cheating on me, and that he was only with me until he finds someone else with more money.

Nice.

Of course my daughter didn't tell me any of this at the time; I think it was too upsetting and she didn't want to cause any more trouble. But it clearly affected her and I think it took her awhile to realize that it simply wasn't true. It took her awhile to figure out that there are bad people in the world.

Bad people.

The really sad part is that for years it appeared that all of these straight friends were on our side. For years, it appeared that they were looking after our best interests. For years, it looked like they were part of our extended family. For years, they told me that they would defend me in a court of law if I ever needed a witness for the kids.

No such luck. I felt like I needed to be wearing a bulletproof vest around them instead.

There wouldn't be anyone who would defend me in court. If that ever happened, I'd be defending myself, journal in hand.

But I have to say that the most shocking disloyalty came from family. I don't know about you, but I expect more from family, at least until proven otherwise.

The worse offender was Christopher's mother's third husband, now ex-husband. They got married right around the time that I met Christopher, and by all accounts this man never accepted our "lifestyle."

I hate the word "lifestyle." It should be banished, as should the word "orientation."

Like many others, the man was friendly and welcoming to our face. I think he even smiled once. But to our backs, he was judgmental and offensive, as were other members of our extended family.

I had a family member who for years refused to put Christopher's name on her Christmas card to us. I got to the point where I wouldn't even open it; I just threw it right into the trash. Merry Christmas.

I always held my grandmother from my father's side as a benchmark. Her name was Sito and although I didn't see her that much through the years, she was very special to me.

When she found out I was gay, she called me. Sito was a woman of few words, and an old-school woman at that. She never called me, ever. We would write letters back and forth; we were pen pals, but she never called me.

I don't know why, but she never called me.

Sito called me when she found out I was gay, literally the next day. All she said was this: "You know, your father has an aunt who's gay. I thought you should know that."

That was it. She never spoke another word on the topic, but in our letters and on our Christmas calls she would always say, "Love to Christopher." That's all she needed to say.

We hadn't seen her a long time, so one year we all went to Niagara Falls to celebrate her 90th birthday. The day we went was the exact same day that Christopher lost his beloved Granny. He found out as we were walking into the airport. He never said a word about it to anyone else that day, but celebrated Sito's big day with our family.

I guess in some ways it was an appropriate way to deal with the news, by spending time with family.

Sito called it the happiest day of her life.

When she was getting ready to leave her party to go home, Sito kept asking for me to bring her to the car. She made a huge fuss that she wanted me to help her get into the front seat.

Everyone was running around the place saying, "Where's Jimmy? Sito wants him to bring her to the car."

So of course I ran. She never asked me to do anything, so I ran to the car.

As I got her into the front seat, kissed her goodnight, and started to close the door, she pulled me in to her face.

"Do you know why I wanted you to put me in the car?"

"No."

"I wanted you to be the last thing I remembered about this night."

She died about a month later, having had the best day of her life.

After she died, my father gave me a package that she had wrapped for me, with a note on the outside:

> *James John Joseph III*
> *Not to be opened until I'm gone.*
> *Love, Sito*

The note was faded from years of sitting in my father's closet. I could barely read it.

When I opened the loosely wrapped and somewhat ripped package that was held together by now-yellowed tape, there was knitted fabric and a handwritten note. I didn't know what it was until I read the note:

> *Dear Jimmy,*
> *This is the sweater I knitted for you when you were born. It's a little worse for carrying around from moving but I want you to have it as a keepsake from me. Your grandfather didn't think it was good enough for his grandson and wouldn't let me send it. I hope you will like it as a keepsake and if you don't you can do whatever you want with it and my feelings won't be hurt. Your grandfather and I both love all of you.*
> > *May God bless all of you.*
> > *All my love, Sito*

The note wasn't dated, but I know she included Christopher and the children when she said "all of you." I never asked my father, because I know in my heart that's what she meant.

What a way to build confidence!

When I came out to my parents, I knew they were struggling with it, but they never laid that on me. They were worried about me, they were worried about the kids, and they were worried about what my ex-wife would do as a result. But they never said a word. Truthfully, I think they were so happy for me to get out of an unhappy situation that being gay was just a part of it.

I felt the same way. Doesn't matter what the situation, family support should be unconditional. I am the same with my children.

That's what I came to expect from family, and that's what I expected from anyone who marries into family. So you can imagine our shock when Christopher's mother's new husband turned out to be so prejudiced.

Of course it took a while to come out, but when it did we certainly felt it. It was the very first night we visited them in their new house in South Carolina. He couldn't even wait twenty-four hours!

We had dropped the kids off at my parents' house in Virginia, and then drove the long way to South Carolina. For some reason that I still have not figured out, what we thought would be a five-hour drive turned out to be a ten-hour drive. This was way before Google maps, so who knows how we did the math.

The very first night we were there, he got drunk, mind-blowingly drunk. Two bites into dinner, he blurted out how he really felt: "You people shouldn't have children."

You people. Children.

We tried to ignore it at first; we didn't want to embarrass Christopher's mother. She had been trying to get us to come visit for a long time, and she had prepared an amazing dinner. She's a fantastic cook, and she'd put together a beautiful outdoor table on the deck.

We were sitting out on their deck in the moonlit summer night, surrounded by candles and flowers. Their house was engulfed by trees of all different shapes and sizes so the setting felt like we were in a tree-house; we were so happy to be visiting them after all these years.

But instead, here we are at another dinner party from hell. What is it about candlelight and idiots that gives them the permission to be so rude?

After he started ordering her around and calling her little names, we realized that we couldn't take it anymore. "You people shouldn't have children." He said it more than twice. We got up from the table, went to bed, and left the next morning.

We didn't see him again until years later when Christopher's sister was getting married and we welcomed him into our home. Christopher's sister came out from New York to have her wedding in Bucks County, so we threw a giant party the night before. *Everyone* was welcome; it was a family event and we welcomed all the family. We also included the groom's parents who, despite enjoying all of our food and beverages, couldn't help but condemn our "lifestyle" afterwards.

Condemn. There's that word again, "lifestyle."

Let me tell you, it's not easy having family in your home that are openly "condemning" who you are, and openly bashing the fact that you have children. It took all I could do to not throw them out, along with all the food they were stuffing in their faces.

It's also not easy spending a fortune for your sister's party, and having everyone throw themselves all over the couple just because they're getting married and just because they're straight. We never said a word.

Now, we had no intention of taking anything away from the bride's big day. We were thrilled that she was getting married and thrilled that we could be such a big part of it. She asked both kids to be in the wedding, Christopher was the "maid of honor," and I walked his mom down the aisle. It was a big day for the family, and having everyone in our home for the rehearsal party was an honor.

But as I thought about it, here's a straight couple who've known each other a short amount of time and because they are straight and decide to get "married," everyone in the family rolls out the red carpet, gets together for a wedding, and showers them with money and gifts. And we have to hear about how some of them don't agree with our "lifestyle." There's that word again.

As parents themselves, seeing their children get married, you would think they'd have some appreciation for us as parents. Even if they couldn't embrace us as gay men, you would think that they could sense our commitment to the children and at least have something positive to say about that. You'd think we'd get a little nod of approval on some level.

We were in no place to say a word at that time, and we would never cause a stir at a family event.

But I'm not sure we'd invite them to *our* wedding.

In the end, who really cares. We had each other, and we had those two precious children…

CHAPTER 16

It Doesn't Have to Match

My daughter has the best hair on the planet.

She's got that big, Julia Roberts-type hair that looks amazing when it's big and curly, and then it also looks long and glamorous when it's blown out straight. She has no idea how lucky she is.

We have the blow dryer and the $250 straightener to prove it.

When she was young, her hair would bunch up into these impossibly huge knots in the back. Sometimes they were so bad that we'd have to cut them out – not that you could really even tell because her hair is that big. We tried all sorts of products to help get a comb through the heavy curls, but really nothing helped very much. It got a little easier as she got older, and today her hair is just gorgeous.

Gorgeous!

She's got one determined head of hair. But it wasn't just her hair that was determined. Since the day she was born, my daughter has been a child with a purpose.

From a very early age, she was incredibly independent and focused. When I would hold her, she would squirm around to get out of my arms and be free. She wanted to be sitting on her own, on her own terms. Sounds strange, but I admired her for that, even in her infancy.

As she got older, this determination took on a different shape: when she decided that she wanted something, she would set her sights and map out a plan. She assumed nothing, and in fact worked hard to make it all happen, not expecting anyone to give her a hand.

She's an independent woman.

Literally the first week she went to college, she decided that she wanted to do a semester abroad in Australia. She even hung a poster of the Sydney Opera House in her dorm room as inspiration. I said go for it. She asked me how it would ever happen, and I said that if she wanted it then it would happen.

It happened. Just like when I went to Cornell.

She attended the University of New South Wales for the spring of her junior year. While she was there, she blossomed as she took on adventure after adventure: skydiving, snorkeling, bungee jumping, and playing with all sorts of animals – in the bars and at the zoos!

The girl always knows what she wants and she's not afraid to say it. She goes for it. This has been true from the very beginning. I used to comment that she always had such strong opinions on everything. "Where do these opinions come from?" I would ask myself.

I actually worried about it a little bit until my J&J friend straightened me out; this the same J&J friend who I invited to the hurried and harried brunch at my house when my daughter was only a few weeks old.

She reminded me that it's much better that my daughter has an opinion than not to care at all. "Do you know how many kids just don't care?" she said to me. Indeed. I never complained about it again.

We used to play this game when she was a little toddler. She was always saying "no" to everything. So I'd start quickly listing out a litany of questions, one right after another, to which she would say "no" to every time, until I broke her down into a joyous laugh.

"Do you want to eat your vegetables?" No.
"Do you want to go take a bath now?" No.
"Do you want to go to bed?" No.
…
"Do you want to have ice cream for dinner?" No.
"Do you want a new car when you turn sixteen?" No.
"Do you want to stay out all night with your friends?" No.
…
"Do you want to say no for me?" No
"You just did!"

She would laugh and laugh hysterically. She laughed every time, but she still said "no" all the time!

In second grade she had her first little boy crush. She went on and on about this little boy in her class. This little boy could do no wrong, and luckily he gave her a lot of attention.

It was nearing Valentine's Day and she wanted to get him a gift. She begged and begged me to take her to CVS where she could buy him a present.

I obliged, not that I could have said "no." I don't even remember what we bought, but I do remember that we wrapped it with bright red wrapping paper, in a box that fit perfectly in her little hand.

After school on Valentine's Day she asked me if I would bring her over to his house so that she could give him the present. Why she couldn't have given it to him at school, I don't recall, but I do remember how the exchange went.

It still makes me laugh hysterically.

Now mind you, she'd been harassing me about getting this gift and bringing it over to this boy's house for several days. The whole way over she was talking and talking and talking about how much he's going to love this present. I was smiling to myself the whole time I was driving.

When we got to the little boy's house she suddenly gets kind of quiet and appears to get cold feet. So cute! She asked me to come to the door with her, which was so unusual of her. She always took charge, even in second grade!

The door opened and it's the little boy's older sister who answered. My daughter didn't say a word so I asked if the little boy was home. Seconds later he showed up to the door with his mom, took one look at us and didn't say a word. Silence, like a deer caught in headlights. My daughter also said nothing.

Two pairs of cold feet now.

Well, this is going nowhere fast, I thought to myself.

I introduced myself and my daughter to the mom, who smiled at me because she knew exactly what's what.

My daughter was standing there frozen with the little red box sitting in the palm of her hands. Not a peep. I went on to say that she had a present for the little boy to celebrate Valentine's Day. The two kids were just standing there in silence.

"You can take the present," I said to the little boy. Wow, it felt like brain surgery!

Complete silence doesn't even explain the two kids, although the mom and I were talking with our eyes as we exchanged darting looks and slight smiles.

I said our goodnights, still standing in the doorway, and I walked back to the car with my daughter.

As soon as we started to pull out of the driveway and pull away, she said to me, "Well, that went pretty well, don't you think?"

What?!?

My heart melted.

As tough and determined as she was, this wasn't the only time she stood frozen in the moment.

We ended up trading up for a larger place along the river in New Hope. We had done well on the real estate transaction the first time around, so we could finally afford to do it right.

While the second place we bought in New Hope was in good shape, it needed some aesthetic tweaks, especially in my daughter's room. The previous owners had used her room as a family room, so the décor was just not right. I wanted her to love her new bedroom.

There was a local furniture store that offered design services so we engaged with the owner and his assistant. We needed some things for the living room and all of the bedrooms. It was a big undertaking for us, but we were up for it.

The designer created mood boards for each of the rooms so that we could decide how to furnish each one. His design services were included with any furniture purchase so it was a good deal. He was a local businessman, and we liked shopping local, although there was no LGD with this one.

He helped us with the living room, my son's bedroom, our bedroom, and my daughter's bedroom too, and we included the kids in all of the decisions so that they could be part of the experience.

In hindsight, some of our choices were too high-end, like the sisal carpet that my son complained scratched his feet and the big, thick, two-sided velvet drapery that the kids used as a theater curtain.

When we got to my daughter's room we figured we'd have the most fun. Girls' rooms are so interesting to decorate, although we weren't going for a typical pink lace look. We wanted a more sophisticated feel that would last as she grew up. She was a very sophisticated girl for her age; remember this is a girl who always knows what she wants. Or so we thought.

At the time, or should I say before this time, red was her favorite color…or at least, that was my perception. So in great earnestness and to really surprise and delight her, we told the designer to do something in red.

His design was very princess-like, although adult princess, and it was very red. Think Lady Diana in red here.

The design featured red wallpaper with a bright gold damask pattern, red bedding with a toile design, red and gold carpeting that had a large floral motif – even red on the interior of a secretary he said we should buy for between her two twin beds.

We were sold and got very excited…probably too excited.

We loved it and she nodded along without really saying too much. She was so shy and demure that we figured that she was just overwhelmed. As Dad, I should have known that something wasn't quite right, but I didn't read her signs that day.

It wasn't until years later that she confessed that she didn't like the color red anymore; she liked purple. She also admitted that she wanted to say something to the designer, but she was afraid to hurt his feelings because he had been so excited. So she took the red bedroom even though red was no longer her favorite color.

Way to go, Dad.

The irony is that red bedding is still in our house! It really is beautiful and has maintained well through the years.

While the decision did indeed stand the test of time and multiple moves, it doesn't change the fact that as a dad I have to listen more carefully, and learn to read between the lines.

One thing she has never been silent about is her choice of clothing.

Whenever we were getting ready for a school event or for a weekend activity, she was always definitive and determined about her clothing. She would mix and match outfits that had no right to be put together. When asked her about her choices, she would simply say, "It doesn't have to match."

One memorable outfit included maroon faux leather pants, a leopard-print hoodie, and cat-shaped glasses. That one was for the record books.

Shopping for clothes was quite easy as a result. We simply pointed out items that she immediately said yes or no to. There was never any hesitation or guesswork. Then when she tried them on, there was another definitive yes or no. She wouldn't even show them to us because she was quite capable of deciding for herself.

Once in a while we would get a sneak peek, to which we would respond with great delight. It doesn't take much to make a dad happy. Christopher is a much better shopper than I am, and it really doesn't take much to make him happy at retail.

One spring break when she was young, she had gone to visit her great grandmother with her mom, and unbeknownst to me got all of her beautiful hair cut during the stay. No one said a word to me.

When I picked her up at the airport, I almost didn't recognize her. Her hair was all chopped off.

It looked adorable, stunning actually, but it wasn't my daughter. Or at least not my view of her – I loved her long hair.

It took me awhile to get used to it, although I didn't say a word. I was a little hurt that no one consulted me first; it's as if I didn't matter. But as long as she was happy with it, then I would try to stay silent. Most dads wouldn't have been involved in the decision anyway; but I wasn't like most dads. It was a lesson in letting go.

The next morning as we were getting ready for school, I mentioned how excited I was to hear what her friends thought of her new cut.

Without giving it much thought at all, she went on to tell me that her real friends would love it. And anyone who didn't love the cut isn't really her friend. Wow.

I thought to myself, *Girl, you are going to need that attitude later in life.* I told my J&J friend and she said, "See what I mean?"

My daughter approaches everything this way, like she is going to make it happen. What I love most about her, even more than her hair or her own sense of style, is the fact that every milestone is a huge milestone.

My daughter makes every turn in life a major event. It's not that she's a drama queen or that she wants to be the center of attention. Quite the contrary, she doesn't seek the limelight at all. It's just that she anticipates every obstacle coming, and she attacks each phase with gusto.

She will kill me for writing this, but this is true even when confronting some of the major milestones in life.

When it was time to start wearing "ladies undergarments" (shall we say), we attacked the situation like it was a school project. I told her that buying bras (sorry!) isn't just about the bra itself, it's about the whole package, so we have to buy matching panties (sorry!) too.

This is where "It doesn't have to match" didn't win…I did! Still makes me LOL.

I didn't know where to go, to tell you the truth, and the stuff at Macy's was hugely expensive. I just couldn't spend that much at the time for garments that weren't even going to fit in six months.

One of the moms from school told me to go to Gap, and sure enough they had a huge selection at their kids' store. This was the one time when we really did get to shop, as we laid out seven matching pairs of bras (sorry!) and panties (sorry!) across one of the store shelves.

It was kind of fun.

We did the same thing when she graduated to Victoria's Secret. We were in Miami on vacation one year and we brought her into the store there to be properly fitted. She had such a look of relief on her face when she finally felt comfortable for the first time in a properly fitted bra (sorry!).

Despite my daughter's potential embarrassment, I have to include these experiences in my story because I never anticipated this part about being a dad, but I have to say it was the BEST part of being a dad.

Many people would ask how I knew what to buy, being a guy and all.

"How do you know what to do?"

I got it: most moms do this stuff. While I understood the question, I didn't grant them an answer. I'm her father after all, so I just figured things out.

I didn't like the implied message in the question, so I didn't want to give it any weight. It was like because I was a man, and because I was gay, then I shouldn't have been involved. It was like they felt bad for my daughter that a guy had to help her with these things, like she was suffering on some level for it. Bastards.

Bras (sorry!) weren't the only uncomfortable topic that we had to tackle.

All of my daughter's girlfriends were starting to get their first period (oh, I'm so sorry!) right before her, so the built up anticipation was more than probably anyone could bear. She was getting more and more anxious.

It got to the point where we had pads and tampons everywhere, just in case "it" came unexpectedly.

We called them breadsticks.

This thing was not going to catch us unprepared, let me tell you. We had them in the car, the bathroom, her backpack, and the kitchen…wherever "it" could possibly strike. It's like we were waiting for an attack from outer space.

We called them breadsticks.

Well, the day finally came, and it came with a vengeance.

I had no idea how severe the cramping and pain would be. I guess I missed that part when we were shown "the movie" in grade school. And I didn't have Google or YouTube to do a quick search.

We were prepared, yet unprepared. Prepared with the breadsticks.

We had heating pads, Midol, an assortment of beverages, multiple flavors of ice cream, and anything else you might need to calm the nerves and settle the body – for her and for me. I also had no idea that it would last a few days.

I ate more ice cream than she did! Christopher just paced downstairs, like we were in a hospital ward or something.

She missed school, and I stayed home from work. This was a life event, after all, not to be taken lightly and certainly not to be dismissed.

Feeling a little inadequate in this department, I had every woman I knew give her a call, including her mom. My daughter needed the support, and I needed the confirmation that we were doing the right thing.

They would talk for a few minutes and then I would hear my daughter say, "Ok, thanks, I love you, goodbye." I would turn to Christopher and say, "That wasn't long enough!"

This from the men who called them breadsticks.

Of course we got through it, as well as every other milestone in a little girl's life including all the "ladies days" (sorry!), first boyfriend, first breakup, college applications, moving into the dorm, and all the triumphs and disappointments along the way.

After all, this is my little girl and I'm her dad. I'm Dad. I can handle the periods and the exclamation points, even if I'm a man.

Now my son, on the other hand, was an entirely different kid…

CHAPTER 17

It's Tradition

"When you say that, it makes me mean."

This is what my son would always say to us when we would be out and about and needed to reprimand him for something. He was a tough kid to reel in sometimes, so we had to stay on top of him at all times. He would just get into "stuff," I can't really explain it any other way.

We had to practice constant behavior modification with my son, but no matter how mad we'd get at him, he always had the ability to disarm us.

We still talk about the constant behavior modification and we still smile about it.

My son was the type of kid who made friends no matter where he went. Whenever we went on vacation, he would end up meeting other kids at the hotel. He'd get into the pool or go to the game room by himself, and he'd come back with a pack of friends.

When we moved to another town as my daughter was entering high school, my son was determined to make new friends in the neighborhood. After living there for a year, he still hadn't met anyone so he consciously decided he was going to change that. He started hanging out at the park nearby our house, and sure enough he met one friend that led to another that led to another. Pretty soon he was having groups of friends over our house on a pretty regular basis. Our house became the social hub where the parents would drop off and pick up their kids to hang out in town together.

He just had a knack for working the system.

Whenever we'd be out and he'd want a snack, like a pretzel or ice cream, he knew all he had to do was say, "Dad, it's tradition," and I'd be sold. I'm big into traditions, big and small, so it got me every time.

We had our favorite ice cream shops, burger joints, pizza parlors, and Auntie Anne's pretzels. Whenever he wanted something, he'd use the "tradition" ploy and he'd get what he wanted. Nothing was ever a big deal, so I always let him win that game. I was a winner too, by the way, because part of the tradition was sharing.

The kid clearly loved his food; I think it was a sign of love for him. To love my son was to feed him.

It's because of him that we started so many food traditions, like spaghetti and meatballs on Sunday nights. Growing up, the kids would have literally eaten pasta every single night. And it would have been easy to give it to them. I can't say that I blame them, I am part of the problem.

When they were really little they even changed the words to the classic Donna Summer song *Hot Stuff*. I actually think they thought that these were the words. Here's their version of the song:

I want some pasta baby this evening
I want some pasta baby tonight
I want some pasta baby this evening
Gotta have some pasta, gotta have it all tonight

So clearly we had to limit our consumption if we were going to have any shot at balanced nutrition.

It was my son's brilliant idea to make it a Sunday night tradition. Brilliant. So now wherever we are on Sunday night, at home or at a restaurant, we have pasta. Spaghetti and meatballs to be exact.

I have to say that I don't take a single meal with my son for granted. There was a day, when he was just a baby, when we could have lost him.

I came home super early one weekday because my daughter had a dance recital and I needed time to get the kids situated, change her clothes, and run over to the school to get her onstage. The babysitter came really early, thankfully, to help feed the kids.

When I walked in the front door, I immediately heard a panicked "Jim?"

come from the babysitter who was in the kitchen.

Let me tell you, a parent can hear panic from a mile away when it is about their kids.

I ran into the kitchen to find my son sitting in his highchair, choking. I don't know what it is about an emergency that sets a parent into motion, but I immediately pulled him out of his chair, told the babysitter to dial 911, and started doing the Heimlich maneuver. I remember from the training that you should hit the baby as hard as you can on his back, if you really want to dislodge the food.

The babysitter immediately had 911 on the phone and was relaying what I was doing to the operator.

I put that baby over my knee and hit his back as hard as I possibly could. I wasn't worried about hurting him; I was worried about getting that food out. He was convulsing and convulsing as I draped him over my leg; I felt like I only had one shot.

Here we go, holy shit, I have to get this right. I raised my arm way back into the air and fired it into his back.

Bam.

That food went flying out of his mouth, and I swear it landed across the room. I think some of it even hit the wall.

But my son kept convulsing. The babysitter asked the 911 operator what to do, and she said to do it again. Holy shit, here we go again.

Bam.

Nothing came out. There was nothing to come out.

Still no response.

Now you would think I would start to panic myself at this point, but I didn't have the chance. The house was filled with an entire emergency crew who just grabbed the baby out of my hands and took over.

That's when I started to shake and panic and sweat. Now I was panicking.

In the end, he was fine.

It turned out that he had a fever that had spiked, right while he was eating. So while I dislodged the food, he was still reacting to the high temperature. Of course the emergency crew figured that out pretty fast, so with a quick trip to the hospital for an ice bath, he was fine. I, on the other hand, was a mess for days. I still shudder when I think about it.

This is clearly the kid that pushes me.

The one thing my son does have in common with his sister is his impatience when it comes to clothes. It's clearly my fault because I'm such a huge clotheshorse; I think it had the opposite effect on the kids. They run away from clothes.

While my daughter says, "It doesn't have to match," my son spends his life in basketball shorts and t-shirts. "It doesn't have to be fancy."

It kills me.

The only time I got him to look even modestly dressed up was when we were on vacation or when we were at a fancy restaurant in New York City. It was my only hope for a collar. Even then it didn't come easily.

One summer we were on vacation in Palm Beach, Florida, at the Breakers. It's a beautiful resort that would normally be way out of our league, but in the summer the rates are cut in half. Florida in August isn't necessarily a draw, but at those rates we were in.

After spending the day at the gorgeous complex of pools, we took a cab into town to do a little shopping. Christopher and I are big shoppers, and although we try to temper it around the kids, we just can't help ourselves. We tried to limit it to just a few hours, with some ice cream thrown in for a reward.

It's tradition. There's nothing more fun for us than buying clothes for the kids.

And in Southern Florida, there's nothing more fun than Lilly Pulitzer for my daughter.

My son is a different story.

We tried so hard to convince him to get a Lacoste polo shirt to wear to dinner that night at the Breakers. We knew he'd look so cute in it and we knew he needed it because the collared shirts we packed for him were all long-sleeved. It was hot and I didn't want him to be uncomfortable.

I even told him he could wear it with a pair of dress shorts. Not basketball shorts but dress shorts. He wasn't having it. He was polite about it, but had no interest in getting a polo shirt; it was too "fancy." Okay, no sweat, he'll wear one of the shirts we brought on the trip.

Well, sure enough, back at the hotel about a half hour before dinner he decided that perhaps he should have gotten the shirt.

While it may seem like he was just being spoiled, in reality he rarely asks for anything. So I jumped at the chance to get it for him. I also wanted the vacation pictures to look nice, and this Lacoste shirt would be adorable on him.

Just to be safe because it was getting late, I called the store to see if they were still open. Sure enough, when the sales associate answered the phone, she informed me that the store had just closed. I saw the disappointment in his face and she must have heard it in my voice.

She asked who she was speaking to, and I told her that I'd been in the store just a few hours earlier with my son. "I thought that was you," she responded with perkiness to her voice.

What?

"Where are you staying?" The Breakers.

"If you tell me what color he wants, I'll bring it over to you on my way home. He's probably a size two, right?" Right.

I was a bit stunned, and my son was thrilled. I told her we'd meet her in front of hotel so that all she had to do was pull up to the curb.

While we were waiting, I of course told him that this was a very unusual thing that was happening. He kept going on and on about how nice she was to do this; he appreciated that she was going out of her way for him. I was happy he got it, so I let him enjoy the moment.

I was so proud of him when she pulled up.

He went right up to the car, and said, "Thank you so much, you didn't have to do that. Thank you." Then on the way back to our room, he apologized to me for not getting the shirt in the store when I had asked him to.

I can't make this stuff up.

A friend of mine was writing a marketing book a few years later, and he was looking for examples of great marketing and surprisingly good customer service. I contributed this story about my son and the Lacoste sales associate to his book.

In that instant, my son learned the best lesson in customer service.

We took a picture that night in the hotel with him wearing that shirt; that picture became the photo for our holiday card that year.

Now that he's in college, he talks about a career in sales and I have to think that the Lacoste experience contributed to his aspirations. He experienced the best, so how could that not influence him?

This coming from a boy who tried every single sport on the planet, every game available at GameStop, and every ice cream flavor, just so he could see what was the best.

We went through the whole cycle of sports, from soccer to baseball to football to lacrosse. While he really was good at all of them, he didn't really enjoy the competitive nature of some of the leagues. He just wanted to spend time with the other kids and hang out. He didn't want to win or lose; he just wanted to play the game.

I couldn't really blame him. I never had that competitive spirit, either; I always wanted everyone to win. Why does someone need to lose? I love every kind of music and I love every kind of sport.

Gossip on the street was that people felt bad for my son because he didn't have a dad that would push him into sports. They said he didn't have a dad to teach him how to play ball.

"Who's going to play catch with the young boy in his backyard?" Give me a break – how insulting.

Now when he was younger, he would cry and cry when one of his favorite sports teams would lose. It was so cute; he would get so upset, inconsolable, even. But it was different when it was about him being on a team. He liked the teamwork, not necessarily the winning or losing part. I respect that about him.

As he got older we talked that he had to focus on one sport if he was going to be good enough to play on a team. He picked lacrosse. He was really good at it right from the start; the kid never dropped the ball!

His first coach was an amazing mentor who really helped my son fall in love with the sport. The coach encouraged teamwork, and he gave each kid a nickname. He called my son "Velcro" because he could always catch the ball no matter what.

My son excelled at lacrosse and really seemed to enjoy it. The coach organized a road trip to a tournament in Maryland every summer, so we would go and stay at a hotel nearby. One year my son and I went alone, one year my daughter and Christopher came, and one year my parents even drove up from Virginia to watch a few of the games.

"Who's going to play ball?" Eat shit.

To keep lacrosse alive all year long, my son even joined the winter leagues and played at an indoor arena before the season started in the spring. He also went to lacrosse camp at Cornell one summer, which was the first time he ever slept away from home on his own. I stayed on campus the first night just to make sure he'd be okay. He had instant friends from the minute he got there. That's the kind of kid he was.

That trip to Cornell ended up being quite special for me. I'm not sure if it was the academic setting or the white wine I drank at the Statler Hotel bar that night, but it was on that trip that I decided to write my first marketing book. I had been thinking about it for years, and finally decided that I just needed to sit down and write it. When I got home, I outlined it all and then researched publishers. Within three months, I had my first book deal.

Soon after its release, the book won a silver medal for Best Marketing Book of the Year from the Axiom Book Awards. I owe that book, that award, and the two sequels that followed to my son and his lacrosse camp at my alma mater.

He continued to play lacrosse year after year and with coach after coach through his junior year in high school. After that, the coaches just got too intense, and it got super competitive. He lost interest when it wasn't fun anymore. He was done.

I loved that he played lacrosse, that is, until he got a concussion. After that I was done too.

I can't blame him for stopping, because the teamwork was gone. The kid just loves being around people, be it his family or his friends. Probably now it's more about his friends, but that's okay; I went through that too.

No matter what I cherished the time we were able to spend together…

CHAPTER 18
A Night Out

"Daaaaad, he won't come out," screams my daughter from inside the maze of tubing at Chuck E. Cheese.

I had just hollered up the tube to tell the kids that it was time to go home. We had been there for hours and I was done. It was Sunday night, and there was school the next day.

"Tell him we have to leave now," I replied.

"Daaaaad, he's stuck," she said.

I guess I'm going in, I thought to myself as I started to crawl through the pit of balls and into the bright red tube.

"Daaaaad!" I heard my daughter scream again as I rounded the first corner of the maze. "He's peeing."

That stopped me dead in my tracks.

That pretty much captures my experience at every kid's birthday party.

The only thing worse than going to Chuck E. Cheese is going in for eye surgery. I take that back, I'd rather stick a needle in my eye than go to Chuck E. Cheese. I know, I've had a needle stuck in my eye.

The ball pit alone killed me. I don't even want to think about what was in those ball pits. I'd get in there with the kids and just sink in. Then it was only a matter of minutes before the kids would start throwing balls at each other and then only a few minutes later when someone would get hit and start crying.

When you're a dad, you do what you have to do, including the ball pits.

When it comes to my kids, I've never met two people who are more different from each other. I swear to you that I treated my daughter and my son no differently from each other as they were growing up, yet they emerged two entirely different people.

For every bit of focused and organized that my daughter is, then my son is loose and carefree. I love them both equally for it.

With crazy schedules and non-stop activities, it was catch-as-catch-can in terms of spending time with each other, especially when you throw in that we split our time with their mom. I'm sure she felt the same way. Most of the time we did things all together, going from event to event. There wasn't a lot of solo time.

Once in a while we would try, though, to give a little dedicated time to each kid so that they could feel super special. We weren't that successful at it, but hey, we tried.

Take, for example, the night we took my daughter out for "date night."

My sister was in town and said that she'd be more than happy to stay home with my son while Christopher and I spent some time with my daughter.

We were living in New Hope, right next door to one of the most unique restaurants in the country: Odette's. It was a restaurant, bar, cabaret, and piano bar all wrapped into one, located in an old stone house right on the Delaware River. We have a lot of great memories from times spent at Odette's.

Because we could literally walk there from our house, Odette's became our social hangout. We would get a babysitter and head over for a few hours and sit at the piano bar. Sometimes we'd grab dinner, and sometimes we'd just sit and listen to the incredible singers. It was a one-of-a-kind place. We often held our big celebrations there as well; we were regulars and they treated us like family. We even had our agency holiday parties there for a few years in a row. It was a slice of life we will never be able to repeat again.

Because we would talk about the people we knew there, my daughter was always begging us to take her. So take her we did, on a "date night" with her Dad and Christopher.

We got all dressed up, because that's what you do on date night. She had this super cute little suit we had bought at Christmas, so she wore that. It was a knitted suit, all black, with a leopard collar and a big kitty cat on it. She looked adorable.

We straightened her hair and pulled it back with one of the dozens of hair accessories that Christopher had bought for her. She had a smile bigger than life that night, as she sat waiting in the living room for us to get ready too.

We were just about ready to head out when we realized that she didn't have a proper pair of shoes to match her outfit.

True to form, the shoes I had bought for her had somehow ended up at her mom's house. I bought all of the clothes and they always ended up at their mom's house for some reason. It made me crazy because I would buy things in preparation for moments like this, and then I couldn't use them.

Christopher could see me getting a little torqued up, so he jumped in. Before I could even think about what he was doing, he grabbed an old pair of my daughter's sneakers, pulled out a can of gold spray paint (I'm not sure from where), and spray-painted them glittery gold. They were amazing; he was amazing. But all I could think to myself was, *Where did he keep that gold spray paint?*

My daughter was beaming with joy as we walked over to Odette's, her now gold sneakers glowing in the dark as we walked along the canal path that ran parallel to the mighty Delaware River. When we walked into the restaurant, she was immediately the belle of the ball. Everyone was wonderful, and gave her so much attention. It was a really special night.

Now, my son was not one to be left out; he wanted his own special treatment. So the next night (my sister was still in town), we did "boys night out."

We put on jeans and our favorite shirts and hit the town of Lambertville, NJ, which is right across the river from New Hope. Although Lambertville is similar to New Hope, the shopping and restaurant scene is very different. It's more about antiques and quiet dining than it is about knick-knacks and bar food.

We boys took off for Lambertville and stopped by an old historic bar called the Boat House, which was filled with sailing memorabilia; it's a real guys' place where you could also sit outside. Bingo.

We sat at a round table and talked about all the things Christopher and I like to do in town. My son was really interested in hearing about what we do when he's not with us. He had quite fascinating questions for us, especially considering his young age. A child's curiosity. I suppose.

We then walked over to our favorite Italian place, called Rick's. Rick's was a Lambertville institution, complete with red-checked table clothes and the best penne vodka for miles. Christopher's sister had her rehearsal dinner there the night before her wedding. It was a regular place for us, so of course my son picked it. It was Sunday night and he wanted spaghetti and meatballs, an institution of his own.

The best part of the entire night was the hat he was wearing to match his shirt. It was white and covered with little images of fish. He looked like a little fisherman, and reminded me of that little boy from the Reach Toothbrush focus group I had met so many years ago. That image of him opening his mouth in front of the "mirror" came rushing back. I smiled inside at how much had changed since then. *(sigh)*

My son, on the other hand, didn't really know how to smile in pictures so he would always just open his mouth wide instead, which made for some very interesting pictures. Adorable, to say the least. *(sigh)*

These moments alone were few and far between, so we cherished every second. Even today, I'll take any available moment alone that I can get. They are even fewer and farther between now.

When my daughter went to college, we had our son to ourselves so we spent a lot more alone time with him. It was usually at home, sitting on our deck just talking until way past dark. Sometimes he was alone, but more often than not, he was with his friends. I miss those nights out on the deck! I guess I should call those "boys' night in!"

Parents' Weekends at college have been such great opportunities to get in a little "date night" with my daughter. I will never forget the first one during her Freshman year. I couldn't believe how much she had grown up in just a few short months. At our first lunch together that Parents' Weekend, we sat at a diner and she walked me through all that had transpired since I dropped her off to move into her dorm. I couldn't believe that this woman sitting in front of me was in fact my little girl! A woman! And to think we called them breadsticks!

I noticed such a change in her attitude toward life. She was so open-minded and eager to explore what life had to offer. We talked about her plans for all four years, because she had already started to map them out. The girl is a planner, and I am so proud of her for that. We talked about a semester abroad in Australia, which I knew even early on that she would make it happen.

But nothing made me happier than when we recently did another "date night" for my daughter's twenty-first birthday. Holy cow. We celebrated in New York with lunch, shopping, a visit to a couple of our favorite "joints," and dinner at the restaurant Buddakan.

Buddakan was featured in the first *Sex in the City* movie, as the place where Carrie and Big held their rehearsal dinner. If you are familiar with the movie, the huge bridal party takes up the center table in the main room of the restaurant. It is wonderfully dramatic and the food is to die for – the best Asian-inspired food in the city, IMHO.

I made sure we got a table in that room, right across from the main table where the movie was filmed. We didn't tell my daughter where we were going, nor did we tell her where we were when we got there. It took her about four seconds to figure it out. It was the best "date night" in years!

With both kids in college, we have to take whatever time we can get now.

I think Sophie felt the same way…

CHAPTER 19
The Baroness

Like many families in America, the kids had been hounding us for years to get a dog. They promised to feed, bathe, walk, and brush it…whatever it took. I think my son even tried to say it was "tradition," knowing that both Christopher and I had dogs growing up.

Yeah right!

We entertained the idea, but at the same time we tried to avoid it. We'd talk about what kind of dog we would get, what we even would name it, and then think about how on earth we would possibly handle it on top of everything else. We knew who'd be doing the walking and the feeding.

Everyone told us not to do it.

The carpets and furniture would get ruined, and we'd be tied down and wouldn't be able to travel. That's the rational part, but the emotion of having a dog always crept back into the debate. Without saying a word to the kids, we slowly started to cave and began researching different breeds.

The truth is that we hadn't gone through the entire range of family pets with the kids, so we were open to getting a dog. We'd resisted the hamsters, rabbits, frogs, goldfish, and hermit crabs. I wasn't having any of that, no way. But a dog? I love dogs!

Christopher started researching and narrowing down our choices, and we decided on either a Pug or a French Bulldog. The kids always picked a Frenchie when he would show them pictures.

I resisted at first because I always fancied myself a "big dog" kind of guy.

Granted, I had a small Poodle growing up, but I always dreamed of having Labs as an adult. I wanted one of each color: a black Labrador, a Golden Retriever, and a chocolate Labrador. Together they would be like an ice cream sundae! I saw those breeds as my kind of dogs.

It was the dead of winter when we were mulling over the choices, so we decided to go to the Westminster Dog Show at Madison Square Garden to help us choose a breed. It would also let us meet some of the breeders and actually see the dogs in action. We made sure we were there when the French Bulldogs and Pugs were on display, because then the breeders would also be backstage. I took a day off from work, that's how important it was to us.

Our plan was set. At this point, because of all the research he had done, Christopher knew some of the breeders by name so it was like going to meet celebrities. We were star struck.

It was love at first sight with the Frenchies. Those stocky little bodies, the bat ears, and the faces just sold us. I wanted one!

They were all sitting, sleeping, and in some cases standing in a row backstage, each with their breeder. It was like a buffet of Frenchies. We knew the kids would be thrilled and we couldn't wait to tell them.

When it came time for the French Bulldogs to show, we went to the edge of the show area to get a good view. We started talking to a woman in front of us who seemed very friendly and also seemed to know a lot about what was going on. This was nothing new for Christopher; he always struck up conversations with people no matter where we went.

Well, it turned out that this woman was the mayor of all Frenchies. She knew all the breeders, and even did interviews for them to help select proper homes for their puppies She quickly became our Frenchie Friend.

Wait a minute! We had to be interviewed to have a Frenchie? No one screened me before I had kids! I guess we passed, because she directed us where to go, who to see, and what to ask, and we really owe a lot to her for helping us get the perfect little puppy.

We went backstage and chatted up the breeders and left determined to get a Frenchie of our own. We also left scratching our heads a bit because we weren't sure if this woman had just screened us or had picked us up. She was that intense.

Over the next few weeks, Christopher followed up with phone calls and pictures with a few of the breeders, all of which had been sanctioned by our new Frenchie Friend. We soft-sounded the idea with the kids, who couldn't have been happier. With the kids in the loop now, the search intensified.

We settled on a breeder from Florida who had a puppy who had just been born. We just had to wait for her to mature a bit, and then we could figure out how to pick her up. She was a fawn (blonde) little girl, perfect in every way.

A credit card swipe later, and it was official.

I will never forget the night we told the kids that we had bought a puppy and that it was actually happening.

My son's response: "Dad, don't tease us unless it's really happening."

Oh, it was really happening. I had paid in full, and let me tell you, those little pups weren't cheap!

My daughter immediately asked when we were getting her, and pulled out a calendar to start mapping out the days. She had a lot to do to get ready for the arrival.

My son said he couldn't wait to tell his friends and wanted to know what her name was.

"Well, that's the best part," I beamed. "We get to name her."

By now I'd learned the kids' differences, so I already had a plan on how I was going to manage the naming of our newest family member. They were both going to want to pick the dog's name, and I had a plan to avoid all the fighting and drama. Fool me once.

They had to jointly pick three names, and they had to decide on the three names together. And then Christopher and I would make the final decision among the names they had chosen. I liked that plan – everybody got a say and we could make sure that we liked the name, too.

Luckily for us, the kids were quite good at selecting names so we had a tough decision on our hands. We had contemplated names like Joan and Betty, names that fit the look of a French Bulldog. We laughed and laughed at some of their suggestions.

The breeder had sent us some pictures, and we ultimately decided on "Lilly," because, well, she just looked like a Lilly.

Now we had to get the house ready with a cage, bed, bowls, toys, and collars. Oh, and piddle pads because we lived in a condo and didn't have a backyard where she could easily do her business.

We also spent time with our Frenchie Friend's dog as well, so that we could get used to walking, feeding, and caring for her. It felt like when I was practicing for when my kids were born.

A few weeks before her arrival, totally out of the blue, I heard from the breeder.

Bad news.

The puppy we selected was born with a problematic back, which is not uncommon with Frenchies. While it wasn't serious at a young age, it would eventually create a lifetime of pain for this little baby. The breeder had to put her down. Put her down?

Noooo!

The news came via email while we were at work, and the breeder said that she didn't have the heart to call us. We had told her all about the kids and she was heartbroken. We were just as heartbroken.

Oh no! First of all, poor little doggie. So sad.

But second of all, what the hell do we tell the kids? How are they ever going to understand? How do we explain it to them?

Not knowing exactly what to do, we called our Frenchie Friend.

"What do we do?!" we shrieked into the phone. "Is Christopher there?" she responded. "Put me on speaker phone."

The first thing she said, in a commanding voice, was, "Don't say a word to the kids. Give me a day and I'll get back to you."

We did exactly what we were told. You don't mess with the Frenchie Friend.

The next day, as promised, we got a phone call from her, and we put her on speaker phone again.

"I found you a dog – a little girl. She's a brindle and she's nine weeks old. She was the runt of the litter so no one wanted her yet, so the breeder decided to keep her. But he's a good friend of mine and he wants you to have her for the kids."

Sold, sight unseen. Frenchie Friend!

The best part is that our Frenchie Friend was planning a visit to the breeder in a couple of weeks so she could bring our dog home for us. The breeder lived in Kentucky, so getting the dog otherwise would have been no easy task. This solved everything.

Now we just had to tell the kids.

It's not like we could just interchange the dogs. They had seen pictures and Lilly was a fawn color. The new dog was brindle, which is a dark brown with blonde highlights, like what you would pay for at a hair salon. We had to tell them the truth. And as hard as it was, this was a good lesson in how life sometimes works.

That night we sat them down for a family meeting and told them about Lilly.

My son was so upset that he had to walk out of the room. We mourned the loss of Lilly for a few minutes before we told them about other news we had received.

I was really impressed with how they handled the whole situation.

It wasn't like the new dog instantly replaced Lilly at all. It wasn't like now she was gone and forgotten. They still talked about Lilly for days and how much they would have loved her. They were very respectful. It brings tears to my eyes now just thinking about it. We would have all loved Lilly.

A day or two went by and we decided we needed to name our new arrival. We needed all new names because Lilly was still Lilly. But we approached it the same way: the kids picked three new names and then Christopher and I made the final decision.

That's when Sophie became our Sophie. Sophie!

We just had to wait a few weeks because Sophie had just been neutered and she had to heal. We could wait, no problem. My daughter crossed off each day from the calendar until Sophie came home.

Our Frenchie Friend was flying back from the breeder in Kentucky, so all we had to do was meet her at Newark Airport to pick up our little Sophie on Sunday night. My son decided to come with me to the airport while my daughter stayed home with Christopher to help get the house ready for the dog.

These were big doings!

My son and I parked the car at the airport, and made our way to the baggage claim. I think we were both holding our breaths and definitely holding hands.

And there she was, in the arms of our Frenchie Friend, waiting for us at the baggage claim at Newark Airport. Little Sophie! Her ears were as big as her head, and her little body was so tiny. She looked a little stunned, sitting perfectly still in the palm of our Frenchie Friend's hands..

Even though we had brought a dog carrier with us, we decided that I would carry her to the car to not scare her anymore. My son carried the bag, and was talking the entire time. Not sure what he was saying, but he was talking the entire time. He suddenly became the biggest chatterbox.

We got to the car after a long march, and put Sophie in the back seat with my son. We sat her in her carrier, but didn't close it. We put her in the middle seat so that she could be close to my son. From that day forward, that is where she sat and slept in the car – right next to my son, leaning up against him from the middle seat.

While we were driving the hour back to the house, my son kept saying how scared she looked. Poor little thing. Her eyes were so big and brown, I'm sure she had no idea what was going on. "Put your hand on top of her so she knows you're there," I said to him.

He did just that and she seemed to calm down.

I'm sure she was used to the contact of her pack mates, and needed to feel a little love. There would be plenty where that came from! My son started rubbing under her neck and she rested her head in his hand. My son melted. Then she licked his hand, to say thanks. While I don't want to exaggerate it, the moment was magical. To this day, my son says how he got Sophie's first kiss.

When we got home, Christopher and my daughter were waiting in the living room for us. We walked in the door and Sophie just sat down and stared at us. She didn't know what to do; we didn't know what to do. We just stared at each other.

After a little time went by, we gave her a tour of the first floor including her food, bed, cage, and piddle pads. She must have thought we were crazy. Almost on cue, she walked into her cage and laid down. It seemed like she was starting to feel at home, which was a signal for us all to go to bed. The next day was a school day.

I felt so bad that the kids had to leave her that next day; they were desperately asking to spend the day at home with Sophie, but I stuck to my guns.

I probably should have caved and let them stay home. Sometimes I was too much of a hard-ass.

They went to school, but I worked from home to make sure Sophie got acclimated. It didn't take long for her to figure out our house and in fact, it didn't take long for her to take over our house. She took over our life, actually. If you have a dog then you know exactly what I mean!

After a few attempts at bringing her to work during the day, we eventually hired a dog walker to take care of her while we were at work. We also hired a trainer to help us get her to learn how to behave.

Just a few easy sessions got us all lined up, including the kids. In fact, I think my son caught on the fastest and was able to make Sophie pay attention the most. He bonded instantly with the training; it must have been that first kiss.

When we had to officially register Sophie, the form asked for her full name. That's when The Baroness Miss Sophie Delight came to life:

> **Baroness**: from *The Sound of Music*, my daughter's favorite movie.
>
> **Miss Sophie**: she was never going to leave us and get married so she had to be a "Miss."
>
> **Delight**: the kids had a favorite ice cream shop in New York called Tasti D-Lite.

The Baroness Miss Sophie Delight.

The joy that this dog has brought to our family through the years is immeasurable. She has slept with each of us, comforted each of us, and yes, irritated each of us. I can't imagine the kids growing up without her.

At one point when she was really young, like two and a half years old, we almost lost her.

We were all in Hawaii on a summer vacation and Sophie was staying at Christopher's sister's house. Long story short, she contracted kennel cough from the dog run in New York, which quickly spread to pneumonia. Bulldogs often have respiratory problems and they can get bad fast.

She got bad fast.

She had to be moved from the vet after several days to a full-service animal hospital. There wasn't a lot they could do for her except keep her comfortable and medicated. She was on a quickly deteriorating downward spiral.

It hit us totally out of the blue, while we were thousands of miles away.

Christopher took a redeye flight home, two days into our vacation in Hawaii, to be with her. He left us to save her life, actually, and to save our family. If he hadn't done that, we would have lost her.

She slowly recovered to her usual self, but only because she got the best care available in New York City, with Christopher literally by her side the entire time. Just like we would do with any of our kids.

That hospital stay created a flurry of health issues, one right after another. The pneumonia set off a breathing issue that could only be addressed with surgery on her nose to open up her air passageway. Only our dog would actually need a nose job!

Years later when moved into the house in Newton, she had such separation anxiety from the old place that she literally made herself sick. That was another batch of hospital stays. We have spent more in health care on that dog than on the entire rest of the family put together. And I would do it again.

Unless you have a dog, there's no way you can possibly understand the impact to your family life. Sophie has been at every birthday celebration, every holiday, every life crisis. There stands our little Sophie, staring up at us, offering her love. My daughter recently commented on her twenty-first birthday that she needed her traditional picture with a birthday cake and Sophie.

There you have it.

Sophie understood everything that was going on.

When one of the kids was sad or in trouble, she paid more attention to them. When we were upset about something, she seemed upset about it too.

Of course, in return, she expected us to know what was going on with her too. She simply stared at us, expecting us to know what she wanted. We generally figured it out, often by trial and error.

Trust me when I say it was Sophie who ruled the roost, not any one of us.

Once the kids went away to college, I always got the feeling that Sophie was looking at the door for the kids to walk back into the house at any minute. Her eyes always pointed to the back door, which is where the kids would come in when they got home.

I felt like I was always looking at the back door too.

I guess in many ways the kids were her pack, our pack. After so many years of the kids and their friends coming in and out of the house, of course she'd be looking for them to come back in. And although she liked her peace and quiet, as do I, she loved it most when the house was full. You could see it in her eyes and in her body language. She wanted everyone around, just like us.

Especially at Christmas…

CHAPTER 20

Photo Op

Christmas: it's the most wonderful time of the year.

You know the saying, "Like a kid at Christmas." Well, that's me.

I love Christmas, always have.

For me, Christmas starts two weeks before Thanksgiving, which is when we start planning our Thanksgiving dinner.

As a kid, I would beg my parents to put up our Christmas tree earlier and earlier every year. Which is why I have no problem when Christopher wants to put the tree up the weekend before Thanksgiving. I'm in!

As a kid I would hand-string garland of popcorn and cranberries to mix in with our ornaments to fill up the tree. Which is why I love that Christopher has the largest collection of Christmas ornaments that I have ever seen. Literally thousands.

Last year we put up seven trees. I kid you not.

As a kid, I would spend hours wrapping my presents so that they would be the most uniquely wrapped boxes under the tree. I learned it from my sister, who is a master at accessorizing. Now I have handed over wrapping duties to Christopher, whose papers, ribbons, bows, and accessories blow us all out of the water.

As a kid was I more about the appetizers than the dinner itself, which is why Christopher puts out a spread of appetizers that would feed the entire New York City Police Department. We eat and drink for hours.

At work, the holiday party is always the most special day of the year for me.

The couple that owned the agency I worked for in Connecticut taught me the wonder of the company holiday party.

To this day, I put a lot of time into planning the party so that everyone has a blast. The theme to last year's company holiday party was "Fire and Ice," complete with food, drinks, and lighting all appropriately hot or cold. Everyone wore blue or red, depending on whether they were "fire" or "ice." I wore a shirt that looked like it was on fire.

This year's holiday party was "Holiday Vegas Style" because what happens at the holiday party stays at the holiday party. My vintage Versace shirt fit the bill perfectly, and it looked great in all the pictures with the Cher impersonator we hired.

It's all about building those holiday memories and relationships, at home and at work.

I love giving holiday surprises; it's one of the joys of life. Which is why we can never fit the presents under just one Christmas tree. It's all about the "wow" and the "unboxing" on Christmas morning.

Christmas was always a very special time at our house, but it was always a little bittersweet, to tell you the truth.

My two kids are the only two kids in the entire family, in either direction. So our house was holiday central, with everyone coming to our place to celebrate. But, being divorced, it came with a price – it always ended too soon because we only had the kids for half the time. Let's face it, Christmas is about the children, so cutting it in half meant cutting the holiday in half.

Glass half empty.

We would alternate Thanksgiving with their mother, one year on, one year off. To compensate on the years we didn't see them on the holiday, we'd have a pre-Thanksgiving dinner. Even still, those years without the kids on the actual Thanksgiving Day were a little too quiet and a little lonely. It made us pause and give thanks, especially for the years when we did have them on the holidays.

Christmas was even trickier for some reason. We would alternate with their mom so that one year they would be with us Christmas Eve and then leave Christmas morning, and then the next year the schedule would flip. While it worked out, it was never enough, not for us.

We'd have an entire crowd in for the holiday, only to be left empty handed when the kids would have to leave. It was the ultimate of highs and lows, which is also why Christopher and I would start so early; we needed to extend the holiday every way possible.

The problem was that everyone would arrange their schedule around the kids' timing, which was fine, except that it left us high and dry when the kids weren't with us and everyone would leave. So we would prepare, clean, shop, cook, and clean again, only to have everyone leave at the same time as the kids. We'd felt like we were left holding the bag. So we had to institute a rule that if you were going to come for the holidays, you had to stay the entire time. If we were in it, then you had to be in it too. A little selfish, I know.

But none of that really mattered, because it was Christmas and me with our family regardless of the amount of time.

Glass half full.

We started a tradition when the kids were really young to kick off the holiday season: a trip to New York for a Broadway show and a really fancy dinner. We saw *Oklahoma!*, *Annie Get Your Gun*, *Mamma Mia!*, and *Phantom of the Opera*, to name a few. We also saw *The Rockettes* more than a few times; the "Multiplying Santas" are my favorite part of the show. They get me every time!

Annie Get Your Gun was the first show we ever saw, with Bernadette Peters playing the lead. It was a special treat from my parents. I kept telling the kids that there was a really famous actress in the show, and that they were really going to love her.

"But how will we know who she is?" my son kept asking.

"Trust me, you will know," I kept saying in return.

As each actor came out, he would ask me if that was her. Nope, but I kept saying that he would know when it's her.

Sure enough, about fifteen minutes into the show, Bernadette Peters made her entrance to thundering applause.

"Ohhhh," he "whispered" loudly into my ear; he was sitting on my lap so that he could see the stage better.

Our seats were way up in the back of the theater; so high that the spotlight for the stage was literally right over our heads. That spotlight proved to be very convenient for him, because he could reach up to stick his jellybeans into the light to see what flavor he was about to enjoy.

Such amazing holiday memories!

Through the years we had dinner at The Four Seasons, Tavern on the Green, and Alain Ducasse, to name a few. But few restaurants compared to La Grenouille in the heart of midtown New York City.

La Grenouille was the first really fancy place we ever took the kids for dinner, so it set a benchmark for many other holiday dinners to come.

While the food was amazing, the restaurant was known for its fresh flowers, which literally filled the air with an intense fragrance at any time of the year, including Christmastime.

With a little trepidation, only because it's so fancy, I made a reservation months ahead. I had never been myself so I was worried it was too fancy even for me. My son kept asking me what it meant for a restaurant to be "fancy."

He would soon find out.

We planned our outfits weeks ahead. My daughter was going to wear a red velvet holiday dress with little black Mary Jane shoes and my son let me pick out a vest and tie ensemble. The two of them were adorable.

As we were approaching the restaurant, I stopped them a half a block away and knelt down in front of them.

"Now remember, this is a really fancy restaurant, the best in the city. You need to really behave and sit up. Don't complain about your food, and be happy with whatever the waiter puts in front of you."

Nothing like being positive, huh?! They were frozen in silence.

We were going to be fine.

When we entered the restaurant, I heard an audible "Oh, wow" come out of my daughter's mouth when she saw all of the flowers.

We were going to be fine.

The place was teeming with flowers, more than I could have possibly imagined; I had never seen so many in one place. I don't know how you can go there if you have allergies; it was just that fragrant. There was no need for any cologne that night, that's for sure.

It was picture-perfect. We were going to be fine.

The waiter took our coats and brought us to our table. It was the fanciest restaurant that I had ever been to, and it blew the kids away. We all stood tall as we walked to the table.

The waiter sat them on the inside banquette so that they could look out. Good call. Christopher and I sat on the outside facing them.

"What should we talk about?" asked my daughter. We were going to be fine, at least until the menus came.

The menu was a bit overwhelming, even for me, and I could see a look of panic start to settle in. There were no chicken fingers and French fries in this joint! I explained to my daughter that when in doubt always order a steak; at least you know what that is. My son asked me to order for him.

When the waiter came over, we ordered steak for both of them. I started to worry a little bit, realizing that there's no way that they'd be able to cut their steak at the table, and also realizing that they were about to get Olympic-sized proportions.

Christopher motioned the waiter over to whisper in his ear so that the kids couldn't hear. I myself could just barely hear him say, "Can you have the kitchen cut up their steaks in the back so that it comes out bite size? Can they split one steak because they'll never be able to eat two portions?" He also told the waiter what sides to include, knowing what would make the kids happy. How did he know this stuff?

When the two individual plates of cut up steak came out for them, each with a small baked potato and steamed asparagus, the look in their eyes was priceless. It's as if they said out loud, "We can do this!"

We were going to be fine.

Dessert consisted of profiteroles (their first ever and one of my personal favorites) and pudding in a cloud (their first ever, and a first for me too). We were going to be fine.

That night at La Grenouille set the standard for every formal Christmas season dinner ever since. We've never been back with the kids, but it's on my bucket list.

For years every time we would go out to dinner, my son would ask if it was going to be "fancy," and then the kids would joke later about where we had dinner and say, "Well, it's no La Grenouille!"

Another year we went to The Four Seasons. For her appetizer, my daughter shockingly ordered the foie grois. The waiter smiled, looked at me for approval, and said, "Of course, the young lady will have foie grois." It's all about the experience. We saw *Music Man* that night.

Another year we went to the new Alain Ducasse restaurant at the Essex House, right off Central Park. It was the most expensive, most controversial restaurant in the city, but we had to try it. It's all about the experience.

When the waiter came over with a clear rectangular deep dish to showcase the truffles for the evening, my daughter reached in to try to take one out. I thought the waiter was going to have a heart attack. It made me smile. That was the night we went to see *Oklahoma!*, the show she had requested for our annual holiday trip that year.

Every restaurant and every show was a new experience, and always with a trip to see the tree at Rockefeller Center squeezed in somehow. I love taking pictures in front of the tree! I used to wonder about it as a kid.

We even did our annual NYC trip for the holiday following 9/11. We needed to show our support for the city at a time when no one was going to New York. I love New York.

OMG, I can't leave out the best part of our New York holiday tradition!

Every year we also did Breakfast with Santa, which consisted of brunch at the restaurant right on the rink of Rockefeller Center with a visit from Santa Claus, and then skating on the rink. None of us are great skaters, to tell you the truth, but circling around on that rink under the circle of flags, the gold statue, and the buildings of Rockefeller Center was nothing short of magical. I probably took more pictures on that rink than anywhere else in New York. Does it get more New York than that? Does it get more holiday than that?!?

I wish we were there right now.

Those holiday weekends broke the bank but they built so many Christmas memories that I didn't care. I'd figure it out in January when the credit card bills would come in. Can't tell you how many years I said, "Fuck it."

I still say "fuck it" when it comes to the holidays. "We'll figure it out in January," was my motto when it came to holiday spending. Looking back, it was worth every penny, especially now that the children aren't children anymore.

There were years that were so financially tight that Christopher and I wouldn't exchange gifts. "We'll exchange gifts next year," was something we said more than a few years. As Dads, that's what you do.

We'd stuff the tree with gifts for the kids, but then give each other something small. That's how you roll when you're parents.

It was hard because we had friends that would shower each other in gifts, and showcase them to us in an obvious display. It was hard to swallow some years. We would also sometimes hear later that people complained about the gifts that we had given them.

Fuck it. Sorry about that, but our kids are the priority.

I'm not sure if it was inspired by La Grenouille or not, but I have to say that Christopher would outdo himself with food at the holidays every year. It was weeks in the making, but it was a solid four days of eating. The day before Christmas Eve would turn into Christmas Eve, would turn into Christmas, which would then turn into the day after Christmas, one delicious meal right after another.

Weeks ahead, Christopher would jam-pack our Christmas trees with his collection of ornaments. He decorated the most beautiful trees that I have ever seen – I would argue that anyone has ever seen. He engulfed them with glass ornaments of every size, shape, color, and theme. Then when they were loaded with beautifully wrapped presents around the base, they made a perfect photo op.

Every year, part of the tradition was to cut down a live tree. Well, that tradition went away the year the Christmas tree fell down three times in a row from the weight of all the ornaments. The following year we switched to artificial and starting doing multiple trees around the house. We have that many ornaments; it was an issue of safety!

One tree was just not enough.

So a new tradition was born: multiple trees, each with a theme. One was all birds, one silver and gold, one all Santas, one all vintage ornaments, etc. I posted them all on Facebook each year!

It was yet another "tradition," as my son would say. But there was another one that was even more delicious…

CHAPTER 21

Which One's Neater?

I think I've established the fact that our holidays are filled with traditions; the kids laugh at me when I repeat myself and they'd surely be laughing right now.

Some of our traditions stick, year after year. Like Christopher's artichoke dip that has become standard fare for any festive occasion. Piping hot, cheesy, creamy, and delicious when spread on little pieces of French baguette.

Some things, though, we only tried once and never dared do again.

Like the year we used the white carpet in our bedroom to send the kids a holiday message.

We knew we'd be replacing the white carpet after the first of the year so Christopher had the brilliant idea to make Santa tracks from the fireplace to the stairs and then down to the kids' room. He wanted to show proof that Santa had come down the chimney to deliver the kids' presents. So he took his Timberland boots and dipped them in the ashes from the fireplace and made tracks across the carpet.

It was actually quite brilliant.

The next morning, it didn't feel so brilliant when my daughter took one look at the tracks and burst into tears. For her, it was proof that someone had been in the house and that was way too scary. We never did the boot tracks again!

That next Easter she burst into tears again the night before Easter Sunday because she was worried that the Easter bunny was coming into the house. No, not such a brilliant idea after all.

Nor were the gingerbread houses.

One year we got two gingerbread house kits for the kids to make their own creations. Christopher made white frosting to use as "glue" and we bought all sorts of candy decorations. It was quite fun.

We helped each of the kids "construct" their houses, but then each was left to their own devices to decorate them. We had no idea that this would instantly turn into a design competition, the likes of which you only see on The Food Network!

My daughter took a more eclectic approach to her decorations with a random mix of colors and shapes with really no rhyme or reason to it. Remember this was the "it doesn't have to match" kid.

My son took a very different approach. His was very linear. Each row of candy had a purpose and a consistency of shape, size, and color. It was the most orderly gingerbread house I had ever seen from a little kid. It looked like one of the Victorian row houses in San Francisco.

Now being the social guy that he is, my son was of course looking for some acceptance of his creation. My daughter was happy in her own little world; happy with the way she made her own gingerbread house, as disorderly as it may have looked. She couldn't have cared less what we thought of it.

My son was eyeing up my daughter's creation, mentally noting what he considered to be far inferior design. His house was so orderly; he just assumed that he won this competition. Now he just had to validate it.

As he put the last row of M&Ms onto the roof, my son asked: "Christopher, which one is your favorite?"

"Oh my gosh, they both are so beautiful, I don't have a favorite," Christopher responded in the most politically correct way.

Without missing a beat, my son asked, "Which one is more colorful?"

"Wow, they are both filled with so many colors, it's impossible to say."

"Which one is more creative?" My son was desperately trying to find an angle where he could get Christopher to admit that his house was better than his sister's house, all with the innocence of childhood and all while nibbling on M&Ms and white frosting.

"They're both super creative," was Christopher's response.

The boy was stumped.

How was he going to win this one? There was a long silence...you could literally hear the wheels turning in his head. He got a little smirk on his face, discovering a way to win this war.

...(drum roll please)...

"Which one's...neater?"

I thought I was going to lose my shit.

I started laughing so hard that I had to leave the room. The only person laughing more than me was Christopher and even my daughter was laughing while finishing up her impressionistic house. Soon my son caught onto the humor of it too and we all laughed and laughed.

We didn't repeat the gingerbread house construction project the next year, for obvious reasons.

Every once in a while, totally out of the blue, I simply say to Christopher, "Which one's neater?" We laugh and laugh.

"Which one's...neater?"

My favorite tradition is one that started in Christopher's childhood; he has carried it forward into our family. I love it because it has a clear objective: great Christmas pictures.

If you think about it, most people take a lot of formal pictures during holidays, when they are all dressed up and ready to party. Christmas morning is unique because we take pictures when we first wake up, run over to the tree, and start opening presents. This is not necessarily the most picture-perfect time...we are all in our pajamas with major bed head!

Hence Christopher's holiday tradition – we open new pajamas Christmas Eve and wear them to bed so that when we wake up in the morning and take pictures, we are all wearing beautiful new PJs. The best part? They all match; boys get one kind and girls get another. One year it was matching nightshirts; another year it was boxers and t-shirts. Anyone who is staying at the house with us for Christmas gets new PJs. Everyone.

It's tradition.

I certainly embraced this one because I'm a sucker for a good picture. I love pictures of friends and family and I love when they're organized and easy to look at on demand. I've got picture albums organized by year in my office at home, so at any given moment I can pull out any year and take a look at what we did.

When the kids were young, it was easy to snap a lot of pictures, but now that they're older it takes a little more creativity to get their permission to snap. But I have my ways.

My daughter must have caught the bug, if the thousands of pictures she has taken during her college years, organized by year on Facebook, are any indication. I'm happy to hand over the tradition to her.

When the kids were super young, I got an amazing tip from a friend at work who was a prop stylist for photo shoots: assemble a chronological Christmas album. She was so sweet and actually bought me a Christmas photo album and told me to put in the best holiday picture from each year. By the time the kids got to in college, I would have eighteen-plus years of holiday photos, organized by year.

I take direction well, especially when it comes to photos. From that day on, I would take a picture from our holiday weekend in New York each year, combined with whatever picture we used for our holiday card that year, and put them in the album.

The holiday photo album is now completely full, over eighteen years' worth of holiday photos, and has become a cherished keepsake. It helps us remember what we did in New York each year, when Sophie came into the picture, and what outfits we were wearing for the holiday festivities.

If I were to get stranded on a desert island and could only bring one thing, I'd bring that Christmas album, without a doubt.

But there's even more holiday cheer where that came from.

Of all the gift gifting, what I loved the most each Christmas is stuffing the stockings. The kids would each get a stocking obviously, as did Christopher and even Sophie. I would try to do a mix of candy, little toiletries, small toy-ish things, and a surprise or two.

There was never anything huge or expensive in there, and that was the point. Little things that made you smile, along with little candies, toiletries, and holiday items. I would pack up the stockings after everyone went to sleep on Christmas Eve, so that they were hanging from the fireplace when everyone got up. Even Sophie liked to sniff around her stocking as one of the kids helped her open up her treats.

It's silly, I know, but it made me happy.

If I could have harnessed the energy of Christmas and used it all year long, I would have done it in a heartbeat. It's the one time of year that I could really unplug from work; it's the one time of year that we could sit around in the family room with a table full of appetizers, music playing over the sound system, with everyone just talking. Just cooking and drinking and eating and talking.

When the kids were younger, they played while the adults did all the talking. It was often my parents trying to figure out if we were okay, if we could handle all the drama, and if we could get through it. As the years went by, it was often us talking to my parents about health issues and if they could handle all the drama, and if they were going to be able to get through it. Now that the kids are older, it's them talking about their plans for the weekend and their plans for after college.

It's the one time of year that we could huddle. We huddled and talked about our lives, separate and apart. It's the one time of year that we just chilled. As the kids got older, and our parents got older too, this time together became more and more vital.

I also think it's the one time of year where we could stop and give each other credit for who we were and what we'd accomplished. I loved that about the holidays.

We certainly should have done it more often…

CHAPTER 22

Absolutely Nothing At All

I don't ever give Christopher enough credit for what he went through all those years.

Imagine being a father by default, but never getting any acknowledgement for it. In fact, imagine getting a whole lot of crap for it from people who really shouldn't have had an opinion and whose opinion really shouldn't have mattered.

He lived the classic "stepparent" role; made no difference that we happen to be gay, the same stuff happened to any stepfather. While our circumstances were different, those feelings of being isolated and often separated as a stepparent are exactly the same.

The law and public opinion certainly didn't support Christopher either... he was never legitimized as a stepparent. So when you don't have society and the people around you acknowledging what you are doing, how do you ever label or describe it? How can you ever be proud of it?

He knowingly stepped into a relationship with kids not knowing at all what that really meant and where it was going to go. That's not easy, on any level.

Was he "Dad," or "Step-Dad," or just Christopher?

He was mostly just Christopher. When we were really comfortable with someone then we would say "our kids" or he would say "my kids." But unless we really knew the person, we were met with very strange looks. The really obnoxious people would literally say to him, "But those aren't your kids."

Someone actually said that to Christopher in *our* home. Okay, so neither of us are perfect but how do you say that to someone who has taken care of two children for years?

I'm sorry, but who are you?

To commemorate the turn of the century in 2000, we decided to have professional photos taken of all of us. When we arrived at the studio, the photographer said to me, "Who's that?" in reference to Christopher.

Just take the fucking picture! This isn't a Johnson's Baby Shampoo ad and no I am not wearing a wedding ring.

For the kids, I'm sure it was hard for them too. I'm Dad. Calling Christopher something like "Uncle" would have been just plain awkward. "My dad's friend," which was sometimes the default label, completely left the family part out. That's okay, it was the easiest choice at the time. I got to the point where I really hated labels, and I still hate them. We didn't have one that we could use.

How could we come "out" and describe ourselves as a family?

It was even hard to put a label on our relationship. "Boyfriend?" No, sounds too temporary, and "lover" is too sexual. "Partner" has a real coldness to it, and it often sounds like a business relationship, especially when you work together. "Significant other?" Ouch. "Better half?" Ugh, so cheesy. My "significant boyfriend better lover partner?" Nothing really worked.

I love the idea of "spouse" or "husband," and while that is acceptable in some situations and in some states now, back then we just couldn't use it…unless we were with other gay people and then the word "husband" showed a real connection.

I hate to say it this way, but straight people would look at us oddly no matter the label. We were living with kids in their world but we couldn't get married or say that we were both parents. Technically at some point a common law marriage should have kicked in, but not for gay people, no matter how long-term and committed the relationship.

A few weeks ago I was at a business lunch with a colleague who I hadn't seen in years and she asked, "How's your husband?" I almost spit out my food. Not because we're not married yet but because no one in a non-gay non-social setting has ever asked me that! It took me a minute to formulate an answer.

Recently a neighbor said to me, "I gave my business card to your husband."

I had to stop to think about who they were talking about! I'm not used to the normalcy of it all quite yet.

Straight people can move seamlessly from a date, to a steady, to a boyfriend, to a fiancé, and then to a husband, with ease…sometimes then to ex-husband. Been there, done that. The labels exist and people are comfortable with them. While gay people in some situations have those options now, Christopher and I never had that luxury. We didn't know what to call ourselves, and the kids didn't know what to call Christopher. We had to just "be," right from the beginning.

It's even worse when you are a stay-at-home "whatever it is that you are." Christopher faced a lot of scrutiny, raised eyebrows, and second glances on that front.

In addition to being label-less at home, he lost any identity with his work, which is something that most men hang their hat on. I'm sure that was a lot harder to handle than he ever acknowledged. Meanwhile, he supported, and in fact pushed, my every career move, and took the brunt of the sacrifices while I was out getting the recognition at work.

The worst part was when we would meet new people and the inevitable question would pop up. Sometimes it was right at the start of the initial conversation, or sometimes people would allow enough time to actually like us and get interested in us before they'd ask.

It would happen with almost every new person we met, especially the women. We'd start chitchatting, and the conversation would inevitably go "there." We could almost smell it coming, it was that predictable.

Here it comes, I feel it coming, and here we go…

"So what do you do?"

Bam. Seems like a reasonable question with a very logical answer.

"I take care of our home and the kids," was Christopher's normal response.

Now the equally inevitable reaction, each and every single fucking time…

"Oh, really? You do what? Why?"

Or worse yet, mostly from the women, "Where's their mom?"

I will never understand why the women were much worse than the men. Maybe it's because the men secretly wished they had the time to spend with their kids too. Or maybe they didn't get it enough to even ask the question.

I think the women felt threatened, if I'm being honest, and they took it out on Christopher.

For some reason, it was always worse when it was among "friends," or at a friend's house. We'd get caught by surprise, I'm not sure why, because we thought we were safe. I guess they figured it was safe enough to say whatever they want.

"So what do you do?"

Or even worse yet, the judgments that came along instead of the questions. "Of course you stay at home"…meaning that he found a sugar daddy to take care of him. Little did any of them know that he was the one taking care of us!

I know it may sound trivial, but this was a real source of tension and stress for him, and as a result for me too. He would get so tense that there were times he would dread meeting new people.

He was always waiting for "the" question.

We literally would brainstorm potential responses from "None of your business" to "Have sex all day long" to "shall I make you a list?"

I always liked "shall I make you a list?" It captured his essence, IMHO.

I'd heard stay-at-home moms make a similar complaint, so it's not like we were alone in this. Stay-at-home moms have a history of facing judgment from every angle. Now I know I'm going to piss off every woman for saying this, but it was much worse for men who were home. In fact I met quite a few stay-at-home dads who faced harsh judgments, so it's not just limited to gay people.

Why on earth would making sure that your kids have a happy and productive childhood be something less than spectacular? I will never understand why people would criticize such a role.

Let me tell you, there were days I was thrilled to go back to work after an exhausting weekend taking care of the kids. Christopher didn't have that luxury.

I did end up having a favorite response to "the" question, one that beat out all the others hands down.

I loved it the first time I heard it, but I can take no credit for its creation. Christopher picked it up from a very cool stay-at-home mom who had coached him on how to handle these idiots. She had witnessed him struggle at a party, so she clued him in on how she handled the same situation. Christopher then debuted this response to a woman who was being totally obnoxious at a party one night where we thought we were amongst friends.

This particular woman was a doozy, asking Christopher question after question about the kids and about me. She was gearing up for the "so what do you do" question and he was gearing up for the answer; I could just tell – but I didn't know what he was going to say this time around. I could see him nodding his head to her droning on and on.

And then it came…

"Soooo what dooooo youuuuuu dooooo, darling?"

I winced when I overheard the "darling" part; it was that obnoxious.

"Nothing, absolutely nothing," was his response.

I almost shit my pants as my jaw dropped to the floor. With pride.

Nothing, absolutely nothing.

She giggled a nervous laugh as he stared bullets into her eyes, challenging her to ask the question again.

"What do you mean? What do you do?" she asked again in desperate hope that maybe he didn't understand her the first time.

Oh, he understood her the first time, that's for sure. He had lots of practice at this point.

"I do nothing, absolutely nothing. I sit around all day long and do nothing. Absolutely nothing at all."

Good answer.

Her line of questioning stopped immediately as she took a big gulp of what was probably very cheap Pinot Grigio.

Meanwhile, here is the man keeping us all together, allowing me to shine in my career, and allowing me to get all the credit for fatherhood.

I was the one getting the promotions and accolades at work, and I was the one getting the gifts on Father's Day, not him. He sat in silence, keeping the home front home. He was doing all the heavy lifting, not me.

I could never have done what Christopher has done all of these years. You should see the man in action. He knows how to decorate the house perfectly, including all the prep needed for a dinner party. He builds relationships with everyone he interacts with, including the grocery clerk, dry cleaner, pharmacist, and all the neighbors. I don't have that kind of patience.

I recently found out that he was doing a lot more than I ever realized. He would often pick up and drop off the kids from their mom's house, which was a huge help for me. And it wasn't always just the kids getting dropped off. He was always sending over extra food and goodies for them there.

Cookies, brownies, lasagna, spaghetti and meatballs; you name it and it accompanied the kids back to their mom's house. Most of the time, I didn't even know he was doing it.

One time when he was picking them up, my son hadn't finished weeding the front lawn of his mom's house. He still had a long way to go, hours probably, and he was told he couldn't leave her house to go to my house until the front was weeded. My son was very upset about it.

What did Christopher do?

He got on his hands and knees in his shorts and Lacoste shirt and helped my son weed the front yard. I'm sure it was the best weeding job ever done. He did it without ever saying a word to me. My son never said a word to me either; it must have been their little secret.

There were many times he went over to her house to help the kids bring the trash out, feed the cats, and take in the mail while she was traveling. We even sent furniture over to the house. He was just as worried about the kids' environment in that house as he was at ours.

I never even knew he did a lot of this until just recently when I was telling his high school friend about writing this book. She started spilling the beans about the things he used to do for the kids. He never took credit for any of it.

This on top of getting up at 5:00 in the morning to help the kids get ready, to make school lunches, to drive them to the school bus, and then to drive me to the train station for my commute into New York. Not every morning, but enough to make anyone crazy.

Did he complain?

Sure, we both did once in a while. He never complained to the kids though. Did he have a meltdown a few times? Sure, we both lost our shit more than once…we're human, but those times were very infrequent. Was his heart always in the right place? Absolutely. Did he bounce back after an upset like any father would?

Absolutely.

The balancing act for Christopher was different because he was not a "dad," so he wasn't allowed to get mad or upset or tense. It's like his emotions didn't count in the equation because he wasn't the "father." He accepted it.

Christopher never got credit for anything he did, certainly not publically. Quite the contrary, people made him feel like there must be something wrong with him that he couldn't maintain a career, so he decided to maintain a home instead. His job, however, was more important than anything I could ever do at work.

Because of Christopher's care at home, my career has gone to a great place and the kids are happily in college. I can honestly say that it wouldn't be the same case without him.

Even a lot of our family and friends don't really get it, except for our parents. They get it, and really appreciate it. They've seen the fruits of his labor, and the results that we've gotten as a family. They understand his role in raising the kids, and the importance that he's had in making my career possible. They know what it takes to make a house a home, and that we are an equal partnership. (There's that word again.)

Our parents have also appreciated the incredible amount of work that comes from hosting a family holiday when you have a spouse like me who is too busy with work to really lend much of a hand at home.

If you think I'm going to bust out *The Wind Beneath My Wings* or *You Light Up My Life*, no worries. A simple "thank you" to my best friend says it all. Thank you, Christopher, you're my best friend. As Queen would say:

You're the best friend
That I ever had
I've been with you such a long time
You're my sunshine

As we enter the next phase of our lives, I'm hoping that Christopher can make up some lost time for himself and find something truly interesting and rewarding to pursue. I hope he can find something just as exhilarating as I have found in my career. I hope that I can be the one supporting him.

He deserves it.

I promise to never make him play another board game ever again. Come to think of it, he never played board games. Even the kids would say, "Christopher doesn't do board games!"

And I promise to never make him go to another amusement park ever again. He endured a hellish Mousetrap ride at Hershey Park when we were sure that the kids would fall out, he suffered through motion sickness from the Big Bad Wolf roller coaster in Williamsburg, Virginia, and he put up with trauma of a 3-D movie at Busch Gardens that terrified my son.

All my son could say to us after the horrible bee scene in the movie was, "I trusted you." He'd been attacked with multiple bee stings as a toddler, so I guess it stirred memories.

"Do you think it'll be scary?" he asked going into the theater.

"No, it'll be fine," I said confidently as we took our seats in the theater.

"I trusted you," my son said, pointing his finger at both of us, rushing back out of the theater in tears.

Never again.

But I do promise Christopher a life of family vacations, and a snow globe from each one…

CHAPTER 23
Snow Globes

Frozen margaritas are my favorite drink and my favorite place to get one is The Rockinghorse in New York. The bar serves *the* best frozen margarita in the city, if not the country. It's all about the straw, and the margaritas there come with big fat oversized straws.

I think I love them so much because frozen margaritas always remind me of being on vacation.

Just like any other family, aside from the holidays, I think we spent the most quality time together when we went on vacation. While we didn't do it all that often, we certainly appreciated it more than the average family because it was very hard to schedule any vacation time at all. We had to work around the kids' mom who always had her own things to do, their school schedules, my work calendar, and then as they got older, we had to factor in their jobs as well.

It's a wonder we were able to ever do anything at all. Getting a week where we could all get off and go away was no small feat.

We never traveled much as a kid, and I've always felt like I missed out on a lot of childhood memories as a result. My parents are just not travelers, and I don't think they could afford it. I understand completely now; family trips are a small fortune!

So I tried as best I could to make up for it with my kids.

Every Fourth of July, almost without fail, we went to visit my parents in Williamsburg, Virginia. I mean, really, is there a better place to celebrate our country's birth?

The kids loved going to see my parents and in fact for many years they would go and stay there by themselves for a week or two. We would meet my parents halfway so that the trip back and forth from northern Pennsylvania to central Virginia wasn't too taxing. It was wonderful for the kids to spend so much time with their grandparents. Children should spend as much alone time as they can with their grandparents; it's nurturing for both generations.

Every Fourth of July we'd go to a private party held at one of the houses within the Colonial Williamsburg complex, complete with white glove bar service and a host of snacks, and of course the best view of the fireworks in town, set to music from the live fife and drum corps. Bravo!

We still go every year; all four of us went just this past summer. It's amazing that we were able to align our schedules, but that's because the kids really wanted us to go. With four adult schedules to manage, we don't know when we will all be able to go again.

Even Sophie was happy to go over the summer.

Although I am sad to say that we didn't play the game Skittle on this road trip. The game goes like this: whenever anyone sees an orange, green, or yellow car they have to shout out "Skittle!" (I think that's the rule.) Of course my son adds all sorts of variations to the game, just to confuse me and then laugh at me about it. Even now Christopher and I will be driving someplace by ourselves and when we see an orange car one of us will say, "Skittle!"

When Christopher's grandparents were around, we went and visited them a few times in California as well. They loved the kids, and the kids loved them. They lived on the side of a mountain, overlooking the richest farmland in the country where they grow not only grapes for wine, but also lettuce, broccoli, and many other vegetables. It's called the "Salad Bowl of the World" for good reason. It's completely rural and totally fabulous.

On the opposite side of the spectrum is South Beach, Miami, and I have probably been there every year since my son was born. It was one of the first "gay" places I went to and I love going back time and time again. Christopher and I decided to bring the kids there one summer, which was a big hit. From South Beach we ventured down to Key West, which wasn't such a highlight.

For years I had heard about the amazing Key West. While it's a long drive from Miami, it's so scenic as you drive through the Everglades and then along the Florida Keys. Key West is at the very end, the southernmost point of the United States.

This part of the trip was a bust because the hotel we stayed at was a dump. DUMP. And the town itself felt more like a college Spring Break destination than a luxury resort town. I may be wrong, but that was our experience.

The worst part? The ants! They were everywhere in our hotel room, and would literally form lines as they crossed over the furniture, through the beds, along the floor, and up the door. It was disgusting. The kids were completely freaked out, and I couldn't blame them. They wouldn't go to bed, they didn't want to stay in town, and they didn't want to do anything. It was a disaster.

Despite pleading with the front desk, and multiple cans of Raid, we just couldn't do anything about it. We had to suffer through.

The first night we were there I had a big fight with the kids, when they wouldn't settle down. They were afraid to go to bed. "Just deal with it," I screamed at them in frustration more from the ants than from them. Clearly not a good photo op. We couldn't wait to leave and we've never been back.

Let's go back to the mountains!

I was a ski fanatic when I was young, so I really wanted the kids to learn how to ski. We made a few trips up to Vermont through the years where they took lessons and Christopher and I hit the slopes too. While it was a long drive, it was worth it; except for the year that my daughter caught some sort of a stomach bug and threw up the entire night before we were coming home and then the entire car trip back; hours and hours of the dry heaves made for a very long ride.

One year we decided to surprise the kids and go to the Trapp Family Lodge in Stowe, Vermont. Stowe is way up north in the state, so it's an even farther ride. If you know the story of *The Sound of Music*, then you know the von Trapp Family. The real family migrated to the United States during the war, and settled in Vermont. They must have felt comfortable in the snowy mountains!

They opened a ski lodge there, and the youngest daughter still operated it at the time. The look on my daughter's face when we pointed out the person playing the piano in the lobby! It was worth every mile of the trip.

Stowe, Vermont is also where my son discovered crème brûlée and chocolate molten lava cake for the first time. Soon enough, Christopher was making it at home for him.

None of the vacations compare, however, to my brilliant idea to start a new tradition. Okay, so it was a tradition that only lasted one time, but it was a brilliant idea nonetheless.

As my daughter started to approach her tenth birthday, I decided that ten years was indeed a milestone – it was enough of a milestone that it needed to be celebrated differently. So I announced that for her tenth birthday, she could plan her birthday trip to anywhere in the world for one week. All she had to do was decide on a place and help me to plan it.

"Are you in?"

Her first-round choices: New York, Boston, Chicago…not exactly what I had in mind.

So I had to add in a few rules.

The rule was that we had to fly to the destination and it had to be some-place that she had never been to before. Plus it had to be worth a week's visit. That cancelled out her first three choices and I figured that it would seal the deal of someplace amazing.

She only had one pick for her second-round: Los Angeles.

Okay, we can live with that.

We actually had a blast in LA because there was something for everyone. Celebrity sightings, plenty of activities to keep us engaged, lots of shopping where we could buy memorabilia, and amazing restaurants to keep the two adults happy as well.

Oh, and SeaWorld was not too far away in San Diego. My daughter loves animals so that was definitely on the list. After visiting where they train the Hollywood animals for movies and television shows the last time we were in California, she put SeaWorld on her must-do list.

We took the kids shopping and my daughter bought the cutest purses and dresses. She was really starting to evolve her sense of style at this point, al-though it still didn't matter if it all matched.

One night, we decided to go to J.Lo's new restaurant, Dolce. I doubt it's still there, but at the time it was hot, hot, hot. The only reason we were able to get in was because we went early in the evening, which was fine because we were still on East Coast time.

Of course we hit a ton of traffic on the way, and the minute we sat down at the table my son asked me to take him to the bathroom. Since he never asks me to do that, I knew something was wrong so I jumped right up.

Christopher immediately asked what I was doing, assuming that I was being over-protective by not letting my son go to the bathroom on his own. "Don't worry about it," I said as I brushed him off.

Sure enough, we took one step into the (thankfully) empty men's room and my son threw up all over the beautiful black marble floor. I think we were the only ones that had been in there all day, because the floor was spotless and proved to be a perfect canvas for his bodily fluids. The mess went all over the place, like a massive Rorschach test.

His first reaction, "Don't tell anyone. I don't want to ruin the night."

"Don't worry, I'll clean it up," I said to him. "Go back to the table and just say that Daddy's going to the bathroom."

I got on my hands and knees in my white Dolce & Gabbana jeans, and "mopped" up the floor with water from the faucet and paper towels from the dispenser. All in a haste before (oh no!) someone walks through the door. I was so happy we'd come early in the evening.

"Everything okay?" Christopher asked as I sat back down at the table. "My stomach's a little upset but I feel better now," I said in return as I winked at my son. His smile said it all, and we had an amazing evening.

Two years later, when my son was turning ten, he started to plan out how he wanted to spend his big birthday.

His top choices: London, Hawaii, Fiji. Clearly he got the concept.

He chose Hawaii, and helped me to pick the island and the hotel, which ended up being the Fairmont Kea Lani on Maui. It was amazing. His itinerary should have cost a fortune, but at this point I had racked up so many American Express points that the airfare and hotel were all covered. Can you believe it? That trip cemented my loyalty to American Express, I can tell you that.

The trip started with a family friend's wedding outside of Los Angeles, and then kicked into gear in Maui. The bride and groom were vacationing in Maui too, so we got to see them a couple of times more on the trip. Nothing like having two gay men and two kids on your honeymoon! Today that would be fashionable and another #PhotoOp.

My son made instant friends with a bunch of other kids at the resort, and my daughter and Christopher explored all the water activities. We ate like kings and soaked up the sun every single day. My daughter went snorkeling with Christopher and got henna tattoos, my son got so close to one little boy that he started hanging out with his family and vice versa.

We were just reminiscing about that little boy the other day, wondering where life has taken him. His dad was also a very active father who had just recently been in a nearly fatal car accident. He had a new lease on life and it showed. He inspired me and I think of him often. He would laugh and laugh as he chased the kids around the multiple pools that were complete with water slides, waterfalls, and diving boards. I think he was the happiest father I had ever seen.

I think about what that little boy's life would have been like if he had lost his father at such a young age. It made me think of my kids and what if they lost their dad at that age. Appreciation.

The resort was massive so there were plenty of restaurants and activities to choose from, so we never had to leave. We forced ourselves to visit the rainforest and to venture to the hotel next door to go to a luau, but otherwise we stayed on the property the entire time.

The biggest drama we faced every day was how many smoothies the kids could drink at the pool. There was a swim-up bar and the kids could not get enough of them. After one day of gluttony, I had to limit them to one every morning and one every afternoon – a rule I broke several times.

We were on vacation, where rules are meant to be broken.

Although Christopher had to rush back home early because Sophie was sick, the rest of us broke up the trip on the way back by stopping in San Francisco to visit his aunt, uncle, and cousin for a couple of days. It was glorious fun, exploring the city with some natives who gave the kids more attention than they could probably handle.

My son couldn't have had a more fitting ten-year birthday celebration and Sophie ended up coming out of what was a pretty critical condition.

For both of their trips, I made photo albums so that the kids could look back on the big trip they had planned. The albums chronicle their tenth-birthday trip from start to finish, because as they say today in social media, "If there's no picture, it didn't happen."

I just made a similar photo album for my daughter to commemorate her junior semester abroad in Australia. I know that pictures are all electronic now, but there's still something very cool about a physical picture album.

While I intended to make the "every ten year" birthday trip a tradition and repeat it every decade, we just couldn't stick with it for my daughter's twentieth. We are all just too busy now. Oh well, we have those memories from ten years ago and they will never fade.

Christopher and I didn't really take many trips on our own all those years; we reserved almost all of our vacation time to be with the kids. We'd try to tack on a few extra days when I'd travel for business, which was always fun but never quite the same.

The only real vacation trips we ever took alone were to Paris for his 30th birthday and then again for my 50th birthday. Now there's a good tradition I hope to repeat. We also spent a week in Florence with both of our sisters to have a little sibling bonding.

We do take one excursion every fall that is our own little personal tradition: a Columbus Day weekend journey up the Hudson River in New York to all the little towns that dot the valley. We do it as a little treat for making it through the year, and we just love it. We have our favorite restaurants and shops, and we've gone so often that the owners recognize us now.

Every couple needs to find a little time to celebrate their relationship and take the time to give each other a hug. Our annual trip up the Hudson Valley is our little hug each year. We've never taken the kids, and in fact, we've never taken anyone. It's our hug, and not for anyone else. Otherwise, vacations were with and for the kids.

But no matter where we went, my favorite part of every trip was the ritual purchasing of the snow globe! Every place we went – every beach, city, theme park, and historical location – we bought a snow globe to commemorate our adventure. It was an adventure just going from store to store to find the right one every time. So now, many trips and theme parks later, we have quite a collection of snow globes from all around the country sitting on display in a black bookcase.

Represented with pride are Hershey Park, Boston, The Jersey Shore, South Beach, and Washington, D.C., among many others. We've got multiple snow globes from all the places in California that we've been to together.

I will tell you one thing though, we didn't get one when we visited the Safari Off-road Adventure one summer. We drove out of that park with our hair on fire after the monkeys flashed us their privates on our windshield and pulled out the molding on the top of the car. "Why does he have a lipstick on his pee-pee?"

Yeah, try to explain that one! There were no snow globes to represent that experience!

I love those snow globes with all my heart, as well as the stacks of photo albums that chronicle all of those times together. Memories!

It's those great memories that get you through the tough times in life…

CHAPTER 24
The "C" Word

I started writing this chapter at a Ruby Tuesday restaurant in a small little town in Pennsylvania where my son is attending college. He and I drove the five hours to get here yesterday, and then spent the day moving him into his new apartment for his sophomore year.

Earlier this same week, in another small town in Pennsylvania, my daughter also moved back into her college apartment for her senior year. Luckily, she is living in the same place as last year, so there's no "moving" on her end. Two big moves in one week would have been hard to take, and by big I mean moving all of their stuff and dealing with my emotions. It's been quite a few weeks of prepping, shopping, packing, sorting, and reminiscing.

With my daughter starting her fourth year and my son starting his second year, I thought it would be easier this time. I thought we'd already been through the empty nest syndrome. But it's far worse this time, I guess because it's not "new" anymore. I'm a mess.

I guess the boy having trouble with the first day of school this year is me!

Last year, with both kids out of the house for the first time, it was all so novel. We were reveling in our "empty-nest-ness" and loving all the texts, pictures, and Parents' Weekends with the kids.

This year there's finality to it all; they are both adults. They are moving on with their lives, and while they still need us, it's very different.

We've also sold our house in Newtown and have moved out.

We've been doing a lot of reflecting back; thinking of all the funny times we laughed and the shared moments together. How ironic that all of this is happening as I write this book. Or maybe it was fate?

The other day I spent hours looking through all of my photo albums.

So many amazing memories, like when the kids were obsessed with sleeping on the reclining chairs when we visited Christopher's grandparents in California.

Until I saw the picture, I totally forgot about the outdoor Easter Egg Hunt at my parent's house in Virginia. My father said he was still finding plastic eggs filled with candy and dollar bills a year later!

Pictures of each Halloween costume reminded me when my son would refuse to wear his costume and used to make me carry it from house to house trick-or-treating.

Best costume goes to the first year I was with Christopher when his mother made a butterfly outfit for my daughter, complete with pink bedazzled wings. We did her makeup to match and both kids made the front page of the local paper that year!

Looking back at multiple years of Prom pictures at our house brought back all the memories of the kids' friends, and made me wonder where they will all end up in life.

I couldn't believe I had actually taken a picture of the gold sneakers that Christopher spray-painted for date night with my daughter. You can't pay for those little moments, nor can you ever get them back again.

But we can't spray paint everything with gold, and we can't just gloss over all of the hard times.

We had our drama as a family, let me tell you, like any family.

With our children, we tend to remember only the good parts. If I weren't writing this book now, I wouldn't be spending any time thinking about any of the bad stuff. Why should I?

As the song *The Way We Were* goes: "it's the laughter we will remember."

I've chosen to forget any of the fights that we may have had at one point or another. It's hard to remember times when things might have ever been strained but they were there.

The fact of the matter is that I'm not a fighter. I don't like to fight. Someone recently asked me the secret of my longevity with Christopher. It's easy – there's nothing ever important enough to fight about. Nothing, absolutely nothing. So I always cave or let it go or he lets it go.

There's nothing important enough to get in the way of our relationship.

I'm kind of that way in all of my relationships. There is rarely anything important enough to fight about. I don't nitpick my friends. And if I have to have a real knockdown drag-out fight with someone, then I would rather walk away from the relationship.

That's just me. It's my way of handling things.

I've been called a lot of things in my life, that's for sure. Creative. Sensitive. Thoughtful. Out-going. Friendly. Empathetic. How very kind of people!

Purposeful. Manipulative. Controlling. Heavy-handed. I own them all!

The one label I can't accept however is "coward," a word that has been used against me several times. It does not apply to me, nor does it really apply to anyone, in my opinion. Each of us has our own way of dealing with our own issues; no one can judge that with a label like "coward."

Yet, I've been called a coward.

To me, "coward" is a "c word" that should never be used, and should only be replaced with "courage." It takes courage to deal with an issue, big or small, public or private.

Is the young man who creates a YouTube video to announce that he's gay after years of hype and speculation a "coward"? No, he has incredible courage.

Maybe it's the context in which the word "coward" has been used against me. I feel like every time I made a mistake, "coward" got pulled out of the closet and thrown in my face.

I think I could accept it as an attempt to get me to understand that I need to confront issues more head on and more directly. I could accept it if "coward" was used as part of constructive feedback, although it's pretty hard to imagine that it could be used that way. It's one of the most negative words in the English language.

"Coward" has been used as a way to push me down, to minimize me, and to diminish what I've gone through. "Coward" has been used as a prejudicial label to make me feel lesser than. Lesser than.

There's no turning back once someone calls you a coward.

To call someone a coward is to strip them of any dignity; it's meant to drop them to their knees, and to take any shred of confidence away from them. It's meant to shut them up and stop them in their tracks.

It's a mean-spirited label and I won't have it. I won't have it.

We all deal with things at our own pace, on our own time. Who is anyone to say what someone else can handle, or what someone else wants to acknowledge or how someone else should have dealt with an issue? Who should ever be allowed to judge how others manage their lives? We each have our own journey; we each have our own story, and I've had to confront my fair share of issues through the years, thank you very much.

I did it the best way I could handle at the time.

I am not implying that I didn't make any mistakes. I made some doozies! I will never say that I am perfect. I made my choices along the way, and I own them.

And I made a lot of mistakes along the way.

Like any family, we had times when we had issues. In hearing stories from other families, I'm not sure any of ours was such a big deal, but to us they were, especially in the moment. Add in factors like a gay couple, a conservative community, and a stressful schedule…no surprise that there were tense times.

But that doesn't make any of us cowards.

Christopher and I both screwed up more than once in a while…how could you not when you are raising kids?

There's no rulebook for being a dad, and we certainly had no guidance in trying to navigate Christopher's role in parenting either. He wasn't a parent, yet he was in a parental role, leaving lots of room for error when handling situations or when trying to remain a quiet bystander. I couldn't have handled it as well as he did, I will tell you that.

He stepped into a lot of shit when we formed our relationship, so it was inevitable that we'd get ourselves in trouble more than a few times through the years.

There were really only two times that he and I had a big fight, and boy, were they biggies.

The first was the weekend of my daughter's First Communion. The entire family was coming into town, and we were rushing around trying to get the apartment ready for guests. We had just ordered a new sofa for the living room, which of course was late. The first time it came weeks earlier and it couldn't fit up the stairs, so we had to send it back to get it refitted into a sectional. It finally come back finished at 4:30pm and everyone was due around 5:00pm.

Without that sectional, there'd be no place for people to sit because we had already given away the worn out furniture we had gotten from my parent's house years ago. We were having a party for my daughter and we not only wanted the house to look good, we wanted people to be comfortable. We cut it way too close.

Granted, we were being irrational perfectionists, but we wanted the event to be memorable for my daughter. The sectional was just the first of many stresses.

We were also hosting my daughter's mom that evening so that it could be a family affair. We were having drinks at our house, and then we were walking over to Odette's next door. Entertaining their mom was always a trigger point. Let's be honest, who wants to spend time with an ex, no matter who they are? It was a source of tension, but we always did it for the kids.

Agree to agree.

This event was a religious occasion, which added a whole different layer of sensitivity. I'm sorry, but it's hard stepping into an institution that denies your right to exist. To get through it, I'd simply channel the grammar school principal as my guardian angel!

No matter what, this was a milestone occasion for my daughter and we were going to celebrate. It was important to her so that meant it was important to us.

We had gone shopping at Bloomingdale's and bought her a real pearl necklace to commemorate the big event, which was Christopher's brilliant idea. Her first piece of keepsake jewelry.

We tried to be gracious hosts for the night, but it was a long night. Suffice it to say that the minute my daughter's mom left after an awkward evening, Christopher's head exploded because I had allowed her to be the center of attention all night. I could have easily not let her take center stage, but I was trying to keep harmony.

As he got madder and madder, and rightfully so, my head started to explode too because I didn't feel like he was supporting me in my efforts to keep the peace.

Oh boy.

We both went off the deep end, resulting in him taking off with his sister with no intention of ever coming back. And I believe I said I wouldn't take him back anyway. Of course an hour later we realized that we were both wrong.

Nothing is ever worth fighting over.

He was in a very awkward position many times like that. Some would say that he didn't have a right to say anything, yet it was his home too and he had every right to feel his own emotions. There were times he would see situations that weren't right, yet he wasn't supposed to act like their father. It's hard to al-ways keep quiet, especially in your own home.

I usually approach these things from a place of calm; kids will be kids and I get that. Sure I would get upset, but I would just handle it and we would all move on. Christopher handles things differently, and tends to react on im-pulse. His emotions run high, that's who he is.

What can I say – this was nothing that any two other parents wouldn't also have to deal with, particularly when one parent is a "step."

But as a gay man, Christopher didn't really have the license to get involved. Or that's how it felt at the time.

I always ended up feeling stuck in the middle, which is probably a result of how I handle things. It's my fault – I like to see both sides, and I like to quickly move on.

Nothing is worth fighting about.

But sometimes you have to fight, and sometimes you have to let it out. I felt like Christopher and the kids were sometimes looking for me to take sides, which was impossible to do. I was always the gate keeper.

Christopher, I'm sure felt like I wasn't hard enough on them and that I didn't support his role in the tough times. The kids, I'm sure, felt like they shouldn't have to hear about this stuff from him and that it was my job alone to discipline.

There was no way I could take sides; that would be a no-win situation.

I always tried to remain the neutral father and partner; I am quite sure that I handled it wrong many times over, with a few meltdowns along the way.

But that didn't make me a coward.

One time I went to pick up my son from his mom's house but he didn't want to leave; he wanted to stay and play basketball with his friends, even though it was dinnertime.

He gave me such attitude, I can't even tell you. I was tired from a full day of work, and I completely flipped out. I pulled him into his mom's house, and read him the riot act about respecting the fact that I had come to pick him up. Although I completely over-reacted, he never pulled that again.

I had one or two blowups like that with my daughter as well, as did Christopher. Mine always seemed to blow over rather quickly, while his upsets created a bit more tension that lasted a little longer. It was just that way, when you're a "step," I guess.

Nothing was easy. In fact the day I tried to finally tell my daughter that I was gay, and try to tell her about Christopher, it was a complete disaster.

Like a stupid jerk, I pulled out the book *Daddy's Roommate* to try to use it as an icebreaker. Big mistake. First of all, she couldn't relate to seeing a book about gay men and according to her she already knew that I was gay. Thankfully I didn't pull out *Heather Has Two Mommies* that I also had sitting by my side. The entire discussion was a bomb.

Not a shining moment for Dad, to say the least, and probably not for my daughter either. I messed that one up for sure.

Bad advice from a therapist…I should have known better.

Her mother later reprimanded me for handling the situation so badly, and for using that book. She felt completely justified slapping me down for not knowing how to deal with it more properly. I took it from her, and didn't say a word, in an attempt to keep the peace.

It really wasn't any of her business.

The truth is that my daughter did already know that I was gay, and I should have just let the conversation be more natural. Both children were growing up with it, on a daily basis, so I didn't need to make it such a big deal. Looking back, I could have used some more advice, but I didn't know who to ask.

Truthfully, I never really had "the big gay talk" with the kids because of that book. It scared me away from ever trying to have a serious talk about it again. Was that a mistake? I'm not sure. I actually spoke at great length about it with a work colleague who was really helpful in sorting it through for me. Her advice was to let it just be organic.

"Why make a big deal about it since the kids have been living with it practically all of their lives?"

Her advice was to create opportunities where they could ask questions, but don't push it on them. Let them ask the questions and keep the answers focused on their questions. Her advice was "don't force it" and "don't make it a big deal." If others are making it a big issue, my best defense was to create a good home.

I am quite sure that she has no idea how meaningful her advice was to me. Sometimes it only takes one little comment from someone to influence how you handle a situation.

I took her advice. Was it the best path forward? I made a bunch of mistakes so I will never know. There's no way it could have ever been perfect, so I did the best I could at the time. As did Christopher.

Was I being a coward? Fuck no.

I liked her advice and used it judiciously for life's big moments, like when my son asked me how a friend of ours got pregnant. My marketing work on the Durex brand came in handy.

Oh boy.

"Do you really want to know?" I asked him. When he said yes, I went down that age-old path of how to make a baby, with him asking me question after question. At each one, I would ask, "Do you really want to know?" He'd say yes, I'd answer, and he'd follow with another question.

"Do you really want to know?" I kept doing that until he said, "Nope." Job done.

There were many times that my son should have asked the same of me, let me tell you. He's never been afraid to tell us about his adventures. I often find myself in situations where I'm thinking to myself, *Do I really want to know? No!*

But to say it didn't get tense at times would be glossing it over. I've been accused many times of glossing things over which is probably true.

Like when I glossed over the fact that we gave away my daughter's bedroom when she went away to college the first year. Christopher's mother had moved in with us after ending her marriage, and she needed refuge. At first she used one of the empty rooms next to our bedroom on the second floor, but when my daughter went away to college that opened up the entire third floor which gave her and us a whole lot more privacy. It made sense to move her up there.

I totally glossed over the fact that my daughter might care about using her room. I sincerely didn't think she'd mind. She loves Christopher's mother, and she wasn't going to be using that room very much now that she was in college. When she was back home she could use the room again, or use one of the bedrooms on the second floor along with the bathroom next to it. I didn't think it would be a big deal.

Over the course of a few months, we took some of her personal things and placed them all in a big plastic tub for safekeeping. I thought it was smart to do that. What an idiot! Big mistake, classic mistake. It was so stupid and I was completely wrong. I not only completely misread how she would feel but I also completely mishandled telling her.

Here I had just finished speaking at a huge industry conference about branding, but I can't talk to my daughter about a simple matter. In that moment you could have literally looked up "horrible father" in the dictionary and you'd see a picture of me smiling like a dumbass. I was so stupid. SO STUPID!

Eventually, after months, she understood and embraced it. If I had handled it better, we could have done things differently. In hindsight, I realize I should have included her in the discussion and included her in deciding how we were going to move things around.

None of us really fought very often, so I don't want to make it bigger than it was either. But it did happen, and there were a lot of very raw emotions running around. I think the difference is that we were in a brand new situation, uncharted territory, where there were no right answers. And there was no book to follow.

We were a family with no precedents, no rules, no role models, and no one to guide us. We were different from everyone else, yet everyone else judged us. Our family was certainly taking the road less traveled.

There were lots of people who would have loved to jump in and say that our "lifestyle" didn't work. They were dying to say that the kids shouldn't be in that "environment."

"You people shouldn't have kids."

I felt like I had to be picture-perfect all of the time. I was afraid that one little upset from the kids would turn into a full battle with a much larger audience.

Like when my son spilled his chocolate milk on the brand new leopard carpet in his room, despite me telling him not to take it in there. I lost my shit.

Or when he spilled hot cocoa all over the kitchen as they were hustling out the door for school.

Like when my daughter informed us that she didn't want to go on vacation with us. Christopher got pissed and left the room. Good move to exit, but still lots of tension.

I wanted to keep the calm; keep everyone happy. I was successful most of the time, but not always. How could anyone be?

There were also just as many upsets on their mother's side as well. I always kept things quiet out of respect, and just hoped that the same respect would be granted in return. For some reason, because it was their mother, it was all just accepted.

"The 'poor mother'…it's just been so very hard for her."

Sure it's been hard for her, but it hasn't been a walk in the park for me either, and certainly not for "the gay boyfriend" who didn't necessarily ask for any of this.

"He's lucky she lets him keep them." OMG

The only fighting that was ever just a little cute was when it was between the kids. My children certainly know how to fight with each other, like most siblings. When they'd be fussing and fighting about something, Christopher would simply say, "YOU take care of YOURSELF, and SHE will take care of HERSELF."

It's a saying that he repeated often.

It worked both ways: "YOU take care of YOURSELF, and HE will take of HIMSELF."

It actually got to be a joke, and they would cover their little ears every time he said it. But it made the point, and always worked to diffuse the situation. I'm not sure that they've quite grown out of it yet, but there's still hope!

Just the other day, my daughter and I were laughing about how Christopher reacts to stuff, and it's almost charming. It is "charming" to me, but I'm more than thrilled that she's grown some understanding about how people are different.

While no one acknowledged it in the past, we are a family, and now we *can* say it out and about.

Now we *will* say it out and about.

I just can't believe how fast the years went by, especially the high school years…

CHAPTER 25
Time Flies, Times Change

I really don't know what happened, but when the kids hit high school it all became a blur.

One minute we were stressing out about picking classes for freshman year and trying to figure out the new high school system, and the next minute we were ordering a cake and reviewing a catering menu for the graduation party four years later.

WTF.

My daughter entered high school as if she was already a senior. She had all four years planned out when she started and she did the same thing when she went to college. As a senior in college now, she's already planning what to do next.

I never really had to worry about her academically; I knew she'd make the most of her experience. After raising your kids for so many years, you start (start!) to understand them inside and out, probably more than they understand themselves at that age.

I know my daughter.

I try to relieve her active mind, and I try to calm her when she gets anxious about future plans. She likes to know what's coming next, which I respect because I'm the same way. When she gets stressed, it's best to jump in and help her plan herself out of it.

A few weeks into freshman year of high school, she asked me if she could stay at her mom's house during the week because it was too hard to go back and forth and her mom's house was closer to the bus stop. She was trying to plan for an easier morning, and I didn't blame her.

Meanwhile, the only reason that her mom's house was closer to the bus stop was because the Catholic high school would only recognize her mom's address as the children's legitimate home, despite the fact that we also had a bus stop right in front of our place. She even had a fellow classmate that lived a few steps away, but she wasn't allowed to take that bus!

I tried to not let it bother me. I said it didn't bother me.

I was not going to make this a big deal.

Deep down I felt like I *was* still paying for being the father, not the mother, and paying for being gay, not straight. Mom was the hero, despite the fact that Dad was leading it all along.

Okay, I'll tell the truth: it killed me, but I carried on.

Interestingly, my son did the same thing when he hit his freshman year, except he opted to stay with us during the week even though we had to drive him to his mom's house every morning at 6:15 to catch the bus for school.

The school still wouldn't let me change his registration so that he could catch the bus that stopped at our house. I tried talking to everyone, including the principal and the head of the busing system. I couldn't break through the red tape, at least not as the father – even after bouncing from person to person, trying to break through to *someone* on the phone.

I wasn't the mother.

So much for joint legal and physical custody.

Here I am being the active father (which most schools beg for), and I am treated like a second-class citizen. The shocking, and kind of hurtful part was how the people reacted when I spoke to them. It was as if the only person that mattered was the mom. They were almost shocked that I would even ask. One person even said to me, "Why isn't the mother calling?"

Go figure. Even in 2009 things hadn't changed that much for us fathers.

As the high school years progressed, discussions with the kids obviously turned more and more adult. The job of dad was less physical at this point; I was sleeping through the night just fine. The job of dad became much more emotional, helping them tackle their issues that were keeping *them* up at night.

As they started to participate in more social relationships, parties, and dating, our conversations turned much more complicated as we would get the scoop on what was going on. I loved every minute of it, because it brought us that much closer. This was familiar territory to me, much more comfortable than changing diapers or making up bottles of formula.

With my kids as young adults, I could handle anything that came their way because I remember having gone through it too. They would have what they needed, when they needed it, emotionally speaking, to help them get through it.

I didn't try to be a best friend, and I didn't buy them everything on their wish list – I couldn't do that even if I wanted. But I did try to be there at every twist and turn, of which there were many.

It was okay that we were not following a more rigid schedule; it didn't matter. The emotional support was now much more important than the physical and I could be there emotionally whenever they needed me. Their preferred method of communication became texting, so I embraced the medium.

My daughter is a texting queen; she was the first in the family to embrace it and she taught the rest of us. The children each got a cell phone when they turned twelve, mostly because I wanted a way to be able to reach them wherever they were. It's important for when they start going off on their own, and it's even more important when you're divorced so that you don't always have to go through the mother.

When texting first started, you had to pay $0.10 each way for each text. Her first texting bill was $1,000!

I learned to embrace texting too, as a quick and easy way to stay in touch. We text all day long, every day, and I have to remind myself to pick up the phone once in a while and call them because they won't naturally call me. To this day when I do see them calling me, I panic a bit…there must be a reason why they are not texting!

I guess you never get over being a parent.

Shopping for prom dresses was perhaps the most fun. I helped my daughter pick out two of the most gorgeous dresses (and all of the accessories) for her Junior and Senior Prom. It was funny to see how the other moms and their daughters looked at me with a bit of awe, or was it ahhhh; not only was I there with my daughter while she tried on dresses, but I had a definitive opinion about each one. Oh, yes, I did.

I know how to shop. She was going to look fabulous, if I was going to be involved.

One of my favorite dresses, to this day, was a canary-yellow strapless dress with a sequined sweetheart neckline and dozens of floor length spiral trimmings hanging from a short skirt. I can't do any justice to it by describing it. You'd have to see it and you'd have to see it on her. It was bright, it was gaudy, it was yellow, and it was big, but there was something about it that made it fabulous. Or potentially fabulous, depending on what we did with it.

On the rack it was hard to even look at, so at first I tried to convince her to leave it hanging there. But she wanted to at least just try it on. I was into the total Prom shopping experience so I said, "Why not."

When she walked out of the dressing room, I didn't quite know what to say. The dress was walking the fine line somewhere between completely hideous to absolutely stunning.

The moms in the shop just looked at me as if to say, "What are you going to say?" It took me a minute to formulate an opinion, because I could have gone either way. I could have easily said "Take it off right now, it's hideous," or I could have easily said "Take it right now, it's a keeper."

It was one of *those* dresses.

The first thing I said to her?

"We need some shoes. We've got to get some amazing shoes if you are going to wear that dress." I turned to the shop owner and asked if there any shoes in the store that she could try on with the dress.

Next thing?

"We need an accessory. I think it needs big earrings to make that dress work, but you can't wear a necklace because it will interfere with all of the sequins." I walked over to the counter and starting browsing through the biggest earrings I could see.

I was trying to think through ways to make sure that it was on the fabulous end of the spectrum, because it had the potential to be really fabulous.

Third thing I said, as I was trying to process where to go with this dress and give her a little direction, "Well, no one else will be wearing it."

I knew for sure that statement would be true because the storeowner kept an inventory of dresses purchased by school and filed them on Facebook for all the girls to review. There will be no duplicates! Smart move.

Finally, I reached my decision.

"Okay, if you are going to wear that dress, then you have to own it. If you don't wear that dress then it'll wear you and we are not going to let that happen. So if you can wear it, then you should get it."

She got it and she got it.

The day of the Prom she looked amazing. I took her to get her hair and makeup done at a salon in town, and she owned it. It was her Senior Prom and it was her night, complete with a canary yellow, free-flowing, sequined dress. All of the pictures she posted online captured the look perfectly.

Of course, my son was in an altogether different place. He didn't care about the Proms, or being organized, or how to get into college…he just wanted to hang with his friends. We were well past the first day of school jitters; he couldn't wait to be with his friends.

He always loved having his friends over.

It all started with his first Halloween party, which became an annual tradition for quite a few years. We had a finished basement in our house at the time, complete with a separate bedroom, television area for an Xbox, pool table, and fridge for snacks and drinks.

We arranged the bedrooms so that each of us could have a little privacy, and the kids could have friends stay in their rooms. His space was the basement. Sophie loved it down there! Although Sophie could go wherever she wanted in the house, it was always the luck of the draw where she would sleep at night.

Sophie's choice was a big thrill each night! A lot of the time she went down to the basement.

One year, he asked if he could have his entire class over for a Halloween party. It was about twenty-five kids in total, so we closed our eyes and said yes.

Christopher decked the house out in Halloween gear, including a decorated Halloween tree, strobe lights, and a dry ice centerpiece for the snack table. If you are going to have a Halloween party, then have a Halloween party! It was such a huge success, that we repeated it every year, year after year until the novelty wore off for the kids. It never wore off for us, so we were sad to see that tradition go away.

Every year we'd be finding Skittles under seat cushions and in corners for weeks!

That first party ignited the stream of friends that then came over to our house all of the time. From that point on, it felt like we always had extra kids in the house, and we loved it. Our only rule was that if you were going to sleep over, you had to tell us so that we knew who was in the house. And also so that we knew how much breakfast to make in the morning!

I miss those days so much!

Time soon came for applying to colleges and we attacked that like we were on a mission.

First up was my daughter, who set her sights high. We visited as many schools as we could, making sure she had everything she needed to make an informed decision. While traveling around the northeast and into Virginia was hard to plan and schedule around everything else, we enjoyed seeing all the campuses and seeing the differences in facilities and in people. There really is a difference; it's amazing.

We soon found out that much of the decision does not lay on us, but on the schools. It is so much more competitive than when I was going through the process…they decide who gets in, not the other way around. If I had been applying to Cornell with her class, there's no way that I would get in, that's for sure!

Penn State ended up being the best choice for her, the first school that she had heard from. Oddly enough, at the very beginning of the process I knew that she should go to Penn State. I could feel it in my bones. And sure enough, it's been a great place for her to thrive.

When it was my son's turn, he was a little less organized but equally as excited to make a good selection. I talked to a couple of friends who all said that Indiana University of Pennsylvania (IUP) would be the best place for him. Oddly enough, as luck (or hard work) would have it, IUP was the first and best place that accepted him. He would be off to IUP.

Interesting to note that both children went to the very first college that accepted them! Fate?

I was thrilled to be at the center of the college review and application process for my kids because I really wanted to guide them to the right place.

I have to admit, I wanted to drive it.

I put my foot down about Catholic colleges this time; they were going to go to a public, diversified school for college. I made two exceptions: Notre Dame or Villa Nova. But in the end, Notre Dame was too far and too remote, and we didn't click with Villa Nova when we visited. Checked that worry off my list.

I knew the kind of experience they would enjoy in college. Each of them differently.

They both ended up going to schools that are perfect for who they are and what they want out of life. Now I know it sounds like maybe I was being manipulative, but I really wasn't. I'm a firm believer that picking the right college is all about finding the right match. No two matches are alike. I was lucky enough to have picked my perfect match with Cornell, and I was determined to do the same with the kids.

I believe we succeeded.

So yes, I overtly managed the process. I knew what it would take to get them the right match, and I made it happen. No apologies; that's what dads do. In the end it was clearly their decision, based on the feedback we received from each of the schools. I just wanted to make sure that they had a good choice in the making.

Success.

BTW, just now, as I'm writing this chapter, I took a break to call my daughter at midnight on the night of her twenty-first birthday just as she's about to start her senior year at college. She's legal, and I'm old! She was on her way to a bar called First where they give you a birthday hat (and probably a free drink) when you turn twenty-one. Of course they do!

I make no apologies for controlling the situation. Their mom let me take control, which made it a whole lot easier for me. I could do what I needed to do on my own terms, on terms that also made it easier for the kids. After years of being out of control, I took the wheel.

I was also noticing a sea change, one that I hadn't expected so soon.

People stopped asking so many questions about me, or at least the questions were taking on a different tone. I started feeling more respected as a father – a good father – and also more respected as a successful businessman who was able to balance it all.

Dare I say it, I was starting to feel respected for who I am.

Being gay was becoming irrelevant, and, well, almost embraced too. "Gay" was starting to come off of the table. Society, or at least my society, was embracing me as a gay man, a gay businessman, and yes…wait for it…a gay father.

Everyone, and I mean everyone, stopped asking me about the mom, which was liberating. Do you have any idea how good that feels?

I had proved that I wasn't a bumblehead or absent dad and I could balance being a father with my own career success.

I had done it.

I hadn't failed like so many were waiting to see. The new folks I was meeting only saw the current state of affairs; they were not privy to the years of struggle during a very different time.

They treated me differently.

There wasn't as much isolation and there were certainly a lot more sincere conversations about the kids, my work, and our home. The tide was changing, and people were starting to understand that gay parenting isn't gay parenting… it's just parenting. Just like gay marriage isn't gay marriage…it's just marriage.

Equality?

"You people" really can have kids.

I have to say, it felt good.

I didn't feel quite as insecure divulging who I was and what my life was about. I started building a confidence that I didn't have before. Maybe it was the times, maybe it was my age, and maybe it was my success. Maybe it's because the kids were older, and I didn't have to worry about it so much. Maybe I didn't have to think about how it might affect them anymore.

I didn't care why, I was just glad that it was happening.

I became much more confidant being "out" at work. I started talking about Christopher and *our* kids as if it's a natural part of who I am and who we are.

Our kids

It *is* a natural part of who I am. It's a natural part of who Christopher is too. And those are *our* kids – that's how we started to talk about them – with confidence. While we are not married yet, we started talking as if we were. I loaded my office with pictures of the kids through the years, including many with Christopher.

Jim and Christopher, and their kids.

Normal? Well not exactly quite yet. But us.

This new form of acceptance became motivating, exhilarating, and freeing for me and for Christopher. I am sure in some ways it was freeing for the kids as well. I certainly hope so.

The best part? I stopped hesitating when asked about my family.

But I still wondered what exactly they said about us...

CHAPTER 26
They Promised, I Asked

Even though we were becoming more accepted in the "community," we still didn't socialize much with people in the area. We just never felt that sure about it, so we spent most of our social time with old friends or in New York. We spent time with people we trusted, and who loved us for who we were.

As my son started getting older, his friends' parents were always dropping off and picking up their kids at our house; we couldn't help but get to know some of the parents as a result. Our interactions with them were taking on a different flavor, and it was now more about us with our kids rather than being divorced or even gay for that matter. They were very lovely people doing great things for their kids, and we were so happy to know them.

My son started bugging us about getting together with one set of parents in particular…their son was one of his best friends. So we finally said "sure" and jotted down their contact information.

It took me weeks to reach out; I was kind of dreading it. I didn't really want to go public as "parents," I guess. Whenever we had done that in the past, it never ended well. We'd become close to people and then we'd find out that they were criticizing us behind our backs. It made us gun shy. We weren't really up for trying it again, but I had promised my son so I had to see it through.

I reached out to the mother of the family, because hey the mothers do all the scheduling, right? Even I can be known to follow stereotypes…shame on me!

She invited us over to their house for drinks. Christopher and I thought that would be perfect because then after two drinks we would have an easy out. If we are having fun, then we could suggest grabbing a bite to eat some place.

From the minute we entered the house, there was an instant connection. We were greeted with big hugs from both of them, and an immediate acknowledgement that their son loves coming over to our house and loves the two of us. Our son felt the same about them, so I knew it was sincere. Their son was indeed a good guy and we loved having him over; he was over a lot! He called it his "home away from home," and that always made us smile.

Funny, because quite a few of my son's friends called our house their "second home," and called us their "second family," but it didn't really sink in until I heard it from one of the parents. I felt very comfortable all of a sudden.

I felt like we had done something right to be able to create such an inviting environment that our kids' friends would want to be with us so much. Well, not with *us* per se, but in our home. I felt very proud all of a sudden.

Well, one drink turned into two and three, and soon enough we found ourselves sitting outside on their patio, next to their pool, in the dark. It had gotten much later than we ever expected to stay. Mind you that at this point in our lives, ten o'clock was late for us! But we didn't want to leave.

We had talked about everything, and quickly realized that we had a lot in common way beyond parenting, although we bonded on the parenting front first.

Feeling very at ease, I dropped the question I'd been dying to ask for years. I told them that the only way I was going to ask them though, was if they promised to tell us the truth, no matter how it would make us feel.

They made that promise, so I asked my question.

"So what do they say about us?" I threw out there.

"What does that mean?" she quickly asked back.

"What do they say about us?" I repeated exactly the same words, assuming that the second time around she would get it.

"I don't understand what you are asking," the dad responded just as sincerely.

"What do the boys say about me and Jim?" Christopher blurted out, knowing exactly what I was trying to find out. "What do they say about us being gay?"

"They don't say anything," she responded. We both just looked at her, I'm sure with our brows wrinkled up.

"They don't say a word about it," he confirmed.

"I don't believe you," I said right back. "It has to come up in conversation."

"It doesn't. They never say a thing about it. The only reason I knew you were gay is because there are two men in the house," she continued. "And of course I also met your ex-wife recently."

"Oh, c'mon," Christopher pleaded, "They have to say something."

"Yeah, they have to say something," I pushed back too.

"Okay," she gave in, "I'll tell you what they say."

Here it comes; I braced myself for the blow.

"Christopher is an amazing cook. There's always food in the house, no matter what time of day. When they sleep over, they sneak into the kitchen when you two are upstairs because they know there's going to be food. You make an amazing country breakfast in the morning. They love to make Christopher laugh. It's like a challenge. They're a little more formal around Jim because he's the dad." It came pouring out of them.

"That's it?" I asked out of shock. "They don't ever say anything about being gay?"

"Nope, it's never come up."

"Have you ever talked to them about us being gay?"

"Why would we need to do that?"

Well, there you have it.

Now I'm still not sure that they were telling the complete truth, to tell you the truth, but I think directionally they were being accurate.

"Oh, and one other thing I need to add," she interrupted herself as she was talking. "Christopher, you really piss off all the other moms because we can't keep up. We can't make brownies like you do. We can't make waffles like you do. We can't, at the drop of a hat, make a plate of nachos because the boys are hungry. It really pisses us off."

Wow!

This generation of youth looks at things differently; they grew up differently, and the parents are changing their outlook as a result.

I'd like to think, in some small way, that Christopher and I are somehow responsible for that with the kids we've grown to love. My hope is that because they know us, we've contributed to their outlook on life.

The absolute truth is that everyone has something that makes them different, not just gay people. Our home has seen friends of every size, shape, color, flavor, and demeanor; every friend is a little different but there are no differences. They seem to have accepted each other for what they each are, and they seem to have accepted us too. Actually, if those parents are right, they don't even think about us.

And to their point, why would they?

It's not just my son's friends; my daughter's friends are much the same way, they just didn't infiltrate our house like the boys did back then. These boys ended up being the fabric of the high school years for my son, and they ended up being the fabric of our home as well. I can't imagine it being home without them. I have a feeling we'll be sticking by them for years to come. The same is true of my daughter's group of friends.

I hope we have them for life.

These same boys helped us move back into a new apartment in New York City after we had left the city for a few years, after a serious financial crash that left us fleeing for our lives. They made going back into the city a festive occasion; they made it something to celebrate after what had been a disaster.

Of course they didn't realize what a help they were at the time, but we did.

In many ways it was these boys who helped us face a very difficult time in our lives, one that almost broke us. They have no idea how much we needed them to be around, in and out of the house, fueling our sense of family.

They have no idea how much they helped me personally face yet another demon…

CHAPTER 27

$0.27

They say that all successful business people go through at least one failure; well this is mine.

I almost didn't include this part in the book; it's that personal.

My friends say I'm brave to include it. I'd feel like a coward if I didn't include it because it was so personally defining as a person, a father, and a spouse. Aside from getting divorced, it's the most shameful time in my life. My head drops down just thinking about it, even now.

I always told myself that if I could make it through those first few years with the kids, then I could make it through anything.

Well, I almost didn't make it through this one. If it hadn't been for Christopher, I'm not sure that I would have.

We got crushed in the real estate market in New York and in Pennsylvania. Crushed. The late 2000s was called "The Great Recession," and for us it was more like "The Great Real Estate Disaster."

We bought our apartment in Manhattan at about the same time that we bought our last house in Newtown. Two real estate transactions at once was too much. We had done well with the prior apartment in The Village, so we "upgraded" to a slightly bigger apartment so that we could have a proper bedroom. It wasn't big by any means, but at least it had a private bedroom so that we could have a little more living space. Space is at a premium in New York, so every extra square foot is a luxury.

At this point, I was working in Manhattan full time, and I needed a place to rest my head. The commute was way too long to do every day, especially when you add late night meetings and client dinners to a non-stop day. To not have a place in Manhattan would have meant not having that job, and I needed to keep progressing my career if we were going to be able to send the kids to college and get what we wanted out of life.

But we still needed "home" to be in Pennsylvania with the kids; there was no way I could have moved them to New York with their mom still in PA.

The problem is that we bought the pre-construction apartment when the market was booming and when interest rates were incredibly low. In the one year that transpired during construction, the market dropped and the rates skyrocketed. We were locked into the purchase, but not into the low interest rate that I had negotiated ahead of time. With a huge, non-refundable deposit at risk, we had no choice but to move ahead.

What was once on paper an affordable mortgage payment now became a nightmare. The numbers had changed by two-fold. Ouch. I had to scramble to make the closing costs, because they too had skyrocketed based on taxes, rates, etc. The *day* before the closing, the day before, the mortgage company called me to say that I needed an extra $25,000 for closing costs. The day before! I didn't have it all, because I was already calculating close to the margins.

I barely made it, only because I took cash advances on my credit cards. I had $0.27 cents in all of our combined accounts when I left the closing for that apartment. $0.27. Thankfully, it was Thursday and I was getting paid that Monday so I could still pay the bills, but those bills were going to close me out again. We had to buy a $35.00 lampshade to replace the one that got damaged in the move and I grimaced as they swiped my card.

I had no cushion. None, zero.

Well…I had $0.27.

I walked out of that closing and back to work like a zombie.

Shortly thereafter, we sold our place in New Hope and bought our new place in nearby Newtown. When we were planning it out, the timing seemed as if it would all work, but the costs of moving and decorating a much larger house strapped us even more. We lost money on the New Hope transaction because the river had flooded three times while we were living there; no one wanted to buy a property that floods. While we were lucky to get out, I still had to sell off all of my stock accounts to raise enough cash.

I had to do it for the kids, and I had to do it to keep my career advancing.

I figured we'd be okay though, because I would get a bonus in the spring. I had done the math, and I'm not a stupid guy; I knew it would work out. I calculated for it to work out.

Through a whole lot of circumstances that weren't fair or equitable, that bonus never came. The economy was so bad that I didn't get a bonus for a few years in a row. There was no relief in sight.

I was still making child support payments and paying for virtually all of the kids' expenses. Remember, "take money out of the equation."

It was money to keep the peace and to stay secure.

Expenses were mounting on all fronts, but I did have a decent salary. There was just no bonus, something I had assumed in the mix and something that would have gotten us right back on track. Never again will I make that assumption. Yes, I should have known better.

Even with the high expenses and no bonus, we were still all right, so I never said a word to Christopher. I had told myself that things always work out, so I figured there was no reason to worry him. I was sweating it out enough for the both of us.

After month after month of mortgage payments that were sky high, I had no choice but to skip a mortgage payment on the apartment in New York. One month skipped led to another led to another.

Shit.

This came at a time when the news, every single day, was flooded with stories about bank foreclosures. The statistics were staggering, and I was on my way to being a statistic.

That's when the incessant phone calls from the bank started. They were constantly hunting me down for payments on a daily basis. It was relentless, and often happened first thing in the morning. What a way to start the day; each call would put me in a full body sweat.

I didn't know what to do, so I applied for help via the mortgage modification program that many banks had started to help people who were having trouble with their mortgages. I was clearly not the only person in this situation. The market had dropped so severely that many people owed more on their mortgage than their house was worth, and I was one of them. The value of the new house in Newtown had dropped too. Many people were simply walking away from their houses, leaving them for the bank to settle out. I didn't want to be one of them.

The thought did cross my mind; a lot of things crossed my mind.

Meanwhile, I was trying to focus on a new campaign we were developing for Nesquik, using the Nesquik Bunny. I needed brain space for being creative, not for being stressed out about finances. I've always been good at focusing, so I just compartmentalized the situation.

I now understand the concept of being under water, because there was no option to sell the apartment given how the market had dropped. I made the mistake of not saying anything to Christopher. I just wanted to handle it; it was my job to handle it. The bills kept coming, the child support payments never ended, and I got deeper and deeper into a hole.

Shit.

One day at the grocery store, Christopher's debit card was denied, forcing him to leave a cart full of groceries sitting at the checkout counter while he ran home to get another credit card. I went back to finish the checkout. He was so humiliated that he never stepped back into that store again, so that he would never have to talk to that particular grocery clerk again.

He was upset because the sales associate looked at him like he shouldn't have loaded up his cart if he couldn't afford it. It was mortifying. When I walked back into the store, they couldn't figure out why a different man had come back to finish the transaction. My explanation fell on deaf ears.

But as Lady Gaga says in her song *The Edge of Glory*, "It isn't hell if every-body knows my name."

I finally had to come clean to Christopher because it was starting to look like we would lose our apartment, despite having applied for help from the bank. They denied me the modification because it wasn't a primary home.

Shit.

After the initial shock, Christopher kicked right into gear. I broke into tears. I completely lost it; he completely started making an action plan.

Man down.

This is what a good, supportive relationship is all about: when one man goes down, the other man rises to the occasion.

I was down and almost out.

To this day, I am so thankful for and proud of him. He never once reprimanded me for getting into the situation and never once reprimanded me for not telling him. He understood on many levels, and now he knew he needed to help me fix it.

"You need to call your parents," he finally said.

Long story short, my parents offered to lend me enough money to keep the bank at bay as we put the apartment up for sale as the market started to improve. It would buy us enough time to try to weigh our options.

But I was still hoping for a reasonable solution from the bank.

I actually formed a bit of a friendship over the phone with one of the debt relief representatives at the bank. I spoke to "John" every week for months as he was trying hard to find a way around the "second home" rule.

He got to know me as a person, and I explained the whole situation about the kids, and Christopher, and about how I needed a place in New York so that I could work the job that was paying the bills.

All I wanted was to lower the interest payment so that I could afford to keep the place. The market rates had dropped, so all I was asking for was a more equitable market rate. "John" got it, but the bank didn't.

He kept calling and calling, and kept trying and trying, and I kept sending more and more paperwork. I sent out massive faxes to him for weeks on end. As this went on for months, he told me not to make any more payments until it was all settled. The backlog got humongous. My shame and stress got overwhelming. Every phone call left me ill at ease that we'd ever find a solution.

We also got behind in our taxes on the Newtown property, so we had threatening mail coming there too. The notices came certified mail that required a signature. One came directly to Christopher on a Saturday morning while I was traveling for work.

Have a happy weekend!

I will never forget when "John" finally called me to say that he'd run out of options. He seemed just as disappointed as I was; I think he feared the worst. I contemplated the worst. I was at the end of my rope, so I had to use the money that my parents offered to lend me.

No nice watch from the Big Sis to get me through this disappointment!

We got through it, with the help of my parents, with the help of Christopher's mother, and with the strength of Christopher. I wouldn't have made it without him. I wouldn't have made it without all of them.

To this day it kills me that we took that loss. If we were selling that same apartment today, we'd be making a huge financial gain. Timing was everything.

It's made me incredibly conservative about anything financial, but it's also given me an appreciation for what we do have.

I take every single credit card swipe as a true gift. I don't take a single lunch for granted. When the phone rings, I still look twice at the caller ID. I look at my kids in college and thank every recognized God on the planet (just in case) for getting them in school and for making sure that they finish, and that I can finish.

I remember that $0.27 like it was yesterday. I need to make sure it never happens again.

But through it all, I learned a lot of things about life and about myself, especially when times get the toughest.

Never throw in the towel. There were days I felt like I should end it all, but I kept going with the hope that I could make it better. Deep down I knew that it was all just money and that's meaningless at the end of the day. I knew I could figure out a way through it.

Let others help you when you are down. I had never asked for help in my life. Not because I'm afraid of people helping me, but because that's not the role I see myself playing. I am supposed to help others, not the other way around. But it's okay; everyone needs help now and then. The help can come from many places, from a stranger you've never actually met to the person sitting next to you every day of your life. Accept the help when you need it.

You never know what people are going through. Cut people a break. I'm sure no one I know thinks that we ever went through a financial disaster. I didn't tell anyone. The kids certainly didn't know and their mom never felt a thing. Now when I see people struggling, I imagine what they might be going through so I try to give them the benefit of the doubt.

Hang on to things that make you happy. Even at the height of my financial desperation, we still did our holiday weekend in New York. That weekend means the world to me, and I just couldn't give it up. We skipped the Broadway Show and the fancy dinner, but we still visited the tree at Rockefeller Center and we still had Breakfast with Santa. The traditions that make you happy have to be there to stay, even if you have to modify them. And I still wore colorful shirts every day, even though I was feeling completely gray inside.

Remember that it always gets better. This was a lesson I had learned when I was going through my divorce. It always gets better. When I was at the worst times of my marriage and coming out, I would remember the advice of a therapist:

Always be honest with yourself, first…
…then be honest with others around you,
as much as they'll let you…
…and remember that it always gets better.

It always gets better. And this was before #ItGetsBetter.

No matter where I go in life, I will never forget feeling that $0.27.

Once we got through it, and we did, I really could see the light at the end of the tunnel. And I finally stopped feeling like I was stuck in the middle of it…

CHAPTER 28

Eighteen, Done.

I had always told myself, "Just wait until the kids are eighteen and then it won't matter."

Through all my doubts and insecurities and fears about being a gay father, I always figured that by the time the kids were adults then I wouldn't have to worry about it anymore.

At eighteen, they could make their own decisions. They could fend for themselves against anyone who might bully them. They would form their own opinions based on eighteen years of being with their dad.

At eighteen, my fears could be behind me.

It's not that I was wishing away the time, quite the contrary. It was more like me looking for some sort of resolution all those years. So it shouldn't have been a surprise to me or to anyone else that as my youngest started to approach eighteen, the frustrations of keeping things quiet all those years would somehow bubble up.

I was ready to blow.

When my daughter hit that milestone, it was a huge accomplishment for her. It was quite thrilling because it was the same day we were moving her into college for her freshman year. Eighteen, a dorm room, a new roommate, and the first time away from home…that was a lot for her to take I am sure.

It was a lot to take for me too.

I cried on and off the entire drive to her college, and then I cried the entire time on the way back home. Just when I thought I had finished crying, a touching song would come on the radio and I'd start crying again. Facebook became my outlet, where I posted pictures and wrote about our fun times together. Everyone's comments back to me really got me through the separation anxiety. My son also kept me busy!

But enough about me – I think the transition was harder for her than she ever let on, but that's my daughter!

Her eighteenth birthday didn't change life that much because her brother was still at home, entering his junior year of high school. We still had all the junior and senior year events with him, which I knew would be a very different experience with him.

My son was born in May so his eighteenth birthday fell right around the same time as his high school graduation, and let me tell you, we were sweating it out. I got him tutors for his entire senior year to help him study and to make sure that he kept his head above water. I don't want to over exaggerate and say that every day was a worry, but certainly every exam caused stress.

My son was staying with us most nights, so it was pretty easy to schedule the tutor and to keep his homework on track. We were doing fine, although without much margin for error.

Towards the end of his last semester, we were down to the wire on a couple of courses, but we were finally feeling like we were in the clear. It was Tuesday night, the Tuesday before graduation, and there was no reason to think we wouldn't make it. I had actually sighed a breath of relief…a bit prematurely, as it turned out.

I was traveling out of town, so he decided to stay at his mom's house and then drive into school the next morning for his last final exam. I'm not sure why, but it felt easier for him that night so of course I didn't question it.

I should have questioned it.

On Wednesday morning, I got up at my usual 5:00am to exercise, write my marketing blog post, and catch up on work email. I had a client meeting at 9:30am, so I was trying to get everything done before all of my meetings got started. By 9:00am, it was smooth sailing. But being a father and managing a stressful career in marketing, I know only too well how all of that can change on a dime.

Or with one phone call.

At 9:20am, just as I was getting ready for my client meeting, my personal cell phone starts to vibrate…it's my son's mom.

This can't be good.

Sure enough, my son had slept through his alarm and missed his final exam. She noticed as she was pulling out of the driveway to go to work, because his car was still there. It was the last final in the last semester, just days before graduation.

Now what do we do?!?

I quickly called him, and he answered the phone saying, "I know, I know." I didn't say a word about sleeping in, because we were now in "fix it" mode. The discussion about how we got to this point could come later.

I would have to be late for my meeting to fix this one. I didn't really need an excuse – I would say it was a family emergency. It was the truth.

Thinking out loud, and knowing how his charm can work wonders, I told him to get ready and get to school. I told him to go to the teacher, be completely humble and honest, and explain what happened…maybe she would cut him a break. *Maybe she'll cut ME a break,* is what I was really thinking.

I swear that I've had this exact nightmare multiple times through my life. I had nightmares about sleeping through an exam, and now it was actually happening to my son.

While he was driving in, I called the school.

They all knew me there, so I figured I would just call and see what our options were. As I got passed from each administrator to another, they each said, "Oh my," and passed me along to the next. I could hear the worry in their voice and I know they could hear the worry in mine.

I finally got to the Principal, who could hear how my worry had turned to panic. She was a lovely woman, one of the main reasons why I enjoyed having the kids go to that particular school. After I told her the situation, there was a long pause of what I can only describe as "comfortable silence" between us. I could tell that she was thinking, which was a good sign.

I let her think in silence so that she could focus.

"Well, we do have a make-up session tomorrow for students who are sick. Since you're son is sick today, he can take the make-up test tomorrow."

Thank you, thank you, THANK you. No really, thank YOU.

In the meantime, my son did indeed drive to school, bolted into his class-room, and worked his magic with his teacher. She let him sit down and take the test, even though at this point he was over two hours late. A lesson learned in kindness.

Thank you, thank you, THANK YOU. No really, thank YOU.

With the drama behind us, we could proceed to graduation and his big ol' party which was held at our house. We had done the same kind of party when my daughter graduated, so we had the cadence down pat. The entire family was coming into town for it, and it would be a big family event for all sides of the family. My parents and sister came for the occasion, as did Christopher's sister and brother-in-law. His mom was living with us so she was party planning right beside us.

The day was amazing, my son was amazing, and it felt amazing to have made it. We hugged the other parents who had made it too; I felt just as proud for the other boys who had graduated as I did for my own son.

He was now eighteen, graduated, and getting ready to go off to college. It was the day I had been waiting for, all the years I was Dad.

Sadly, I had to run off to Indonesia for work the night of his party to do some branding work for our largest global client. It was my second time there, and the work we were doing to build their brand was some of the most chal-lenging of my career. I loved it, but not on the night of my son's graduation.

So while I was there for all of the festivities, I didn't get to participate in all the party afterglow and chitchat. My parents were still there until the next day, so they stayed with Christopher and the kids and got to relive the party the next day.

It's always so much fun to talk about everything the next day, to look at pictures on our phones, and to replay all of the conversations. In many ways that's the fun part, and in many ways that's the therapeutic part. In many ways, I could have used that part. Instead, I was on an eighteen-hour flight to Hong Kong, and then onto Indonesia.

Eighteen.

So when I returned on Friday of that week, I had some catching up to do. Sure it was a tough week at work, especially with all of the travel, but I came back relatively rested from sleeping on the planes and energized to start life with now two high school graduates.

I wanted hear what had been going on, to make up for my lost week.

Of course, as is typical with kids, I got no details from my son. But I knew I could get some juice from Christopher and his mom, because they were in the thick of it and they also spent a lot of time with the extended family.

My son went out for the night; it was a Friday after all. As the three of us were sitting in the living room, drinking wine and talking about the party, I started realizing that I had indeed made the eighteen-year mark.

It hit me like a ton of bricks.

Eighteen years, come and gone. Now my second kid was going to college and I was in the clear. The child support payments were done, as was the need to check in with their mom.

I was done.

I had made it, and so had Christopher. And with his mom living with us the past few years, she had made it too. She was also cooking meals, running errands, and driving the kids. She was wonderful about it all.

While I was reveling in the newfound freedom, I also started getting increasingly angry at having to live with the fears and insecurities all of these years, when in fact I was a damn good father.

Why should I have wasted any time feeling bad all those years?

Why was I "required" to keep my mouth shut all along, for fear of causing an uproar that would have horrible ramifications? Why was I ever in a position to have to doubt my role and my security? Why did I have to take all the blame and bear all the responsibility?

I acknowledged, really for the first time, just how unfair it all was.

I started getting all riled up, fueled by a week of travel and a few glasses of wine. Christopher and his mom kept trying to change the subject, and kept trying to focus on the positive.

But I had to let it all out. I let it all out.

I finally started listening, and finally started realizing where I was sitting. I was in the comfort of our beautiful living room, having appetizers and drinking delicious wine with Christopher and his mother, with Sophie sleeping by my side...so I eventually let it go.

But not before I had a bit of a meltdown first, closing a few chapters from some very difficult times in my life.

Both kids were over eighteen, so it didn't matter anymore.

Eighteen years of struggle were over. Eighteen years of picking up and dropping off the kids at their activities and friends' houses. Eighteen years of dinners, shopping for school supplies, and doing homework. Eighteen years of doing laundry, making school lunches, and driving the kids to school – and then doing a commute to work.

It was eighteen years of pulling in and out of her driveway.

It was eighteen years of the first day of school.

It was eighteen years of feeling like the other shoe was somehow going to drop.

Eighteen years of wondering how I was going to cope. Eighteen years of feeling like I was carrying most of the burden, yet getting none of the credit.

It wasn't going to be about any of that anymore.

It was done; it was over. I was finished.

I wasn't finished being a dad, I was just finished worrying about it all the time. Now I could really just concentrate on being there emotionally for my kids as they start to map out their lives. That's what our lives were going to be about from now on.

I would never worry about "what if" again…

CHAPTER 29

No More If

You know, when your children are young so much of life is conditional and situational.

You live from moment to moment, sometimes wondering how you'll survive. While the best-laid plans might make you feel like you're being proactive in your approach to parenting, things rarely play out the way you've intended.

From the minute they are born, the little buggers are completely dependent on you for all the necessities of life. Food, warmth, shelter. As a parent, we are immediately thrust, unprepared, into supplying the demands of a newborn. Most of us are inexperienced at the start, especially with the first child, but we deal with the situation and somehow get through it.

Through the years, we live through each scenario as our children advance through their development. Every year is a little different, and every child is different so it keeps us on our toes.

Some days we just hope we don't drop them on their head, or mess up their head.

We move speedily, although not effortlessly, from kindergarten, to fifth grade, to eighth grade graduation, to dating, to helping find part-time work, to filling out college applications…we move from situation to situation offering support as they need it in the moment.

We help them get through it, successfully. At least that's our hope, as we tackle each obstacle as if it's our own.

That's not to say that life is a series of one-offs, there is a master plan to make sure they pursue their own happiness. But as parents, our support is based on the specific conditions that we are dealing with at the time.

Now as a parent of two "adult" children, life changes pretty drastically. The kind of support I offer them now is very different. It's far less "conditional" and "situational."

Their problems aren't my problems anymore.

They have to make their own decisions and they have to deal with the ramifications of those decisions. Independently. I'm only there to perhaps provide information, maybe give an opinion, but definitely to offer unconditional support.

No strings attached.

I can no longer say "if." If you eat your vegetables, then you can have dessert. If you get good grades, you can get an Xbox. If you clean up your room, you can go out and meet your friends.

There is no more "if."

Suddenly at eighteen, it all changes. It's not an easy switch to flip, let me tell you, but every parent has to flip it.

As young adults, their issues are far bigger than changing a dirty diaper, getting a school project done, or staying home with them with a cold.

I can't fix the problems they face now; all I can do is be there to help them through them. I can give them guidance, but I can't take the problems away. I can tell them what I would do if I were in the situation, or what I've done in similar situations, but I can't make them do anything.

I also can't get too involved either. And I certainly can't ask too many questions. Dad can get really annoying, really quickly, when you're an adult and you don't really need him telling you what to do anymore. My kids want a different kind of dad. They want a "yes" dad instead of an "if" dad.

They want a "how can I help" dad.

They want their dad to just listen to them, on their terms, and once in a while give some advice and guidance…but only when they ask.

That's the kind of dad I want to be now.

I have to know the difference between caring enough to show support but also letting it all go and letting them decide. I have to know where the invisible line is between managing the situation and just advising on it.

In this way, my life is no different than any other active, caring parent – male or female, gay or straight – we all go through this when our children become adults.

Life has changed. The biggest thing I can do for the kids is just be there for them. No judgments, no conditions, no questions asked. Just love and support.

No conditions…just support.

Especially when they face the questions that I used to get…

CHAPTER 30
The Greatest Gift

When I started writing this book, I was sure that a father's job was to care for his children's emotional and physical wellbeing. It was the first thought I had in telling my story. I feel very strongly about it and I have not changed my mind. But I have evolved my thinking as my book has taken shape, and as my role as a father has changed through the years.

I have to be honest about something that has taken me completely by surprise: as I have written each chapter, I cried at the end, one by one. As I would go through and edit each chapter again, I cried again. As I've described the book to Christopher while writing it, I started to cry each time.

I've been crying like a little baby during the entire writing process. Especially when I think about all of those holidays together.

Each chapter reflects a different aspect of my personal journey as a father and of our family's life together. Reliving each nuance has been wonderful, even the bad parts.

I'm not crying because it makes me sad, and not because I'm not worried any longer. I'm crying because I've evolved, because we've evolved, and because the world has evolved.

I'm realizing how much we have all changed and how much we have all grown. It's not just the kids who have grown up.

I realize now towards the end of writing the book that my perspective as a father has changed along the way. Compared to those early years, "taking care" of the kids is much less physical than it used to be, and it's even less emotional.

Fatherhood is not about their physical and emotional wellbeing any more. Now it's about building their confidence:

Confidence to take on the world and tackle tough situations.

Confidence to know what they want and how to go after it.

Confidence to push off the detractors that come their way.

Confidence to challenge the norms that push people to do things that don't make them happy.

Confidence that comes from a family that loves you no matter the situation, regardless of the condition.

In my children's case, the confidence to say that you were raised by a gay father.

I've learned through this process that this is a father's job: to build confidence. It is a job I will hold for the rest of my life.

No matter how many marketing campaigns I develop, and no matter how many books I write, there is nothing more important than fostering confidence in my children. My goal is to build greater confidence in my children than I had in myself.

Back when I was getting married and having children, there were very few visibly gay people. I really didn't know any at all, and certainly didn't know any growing up.

When I was going through a divorce with two very young children and coming out as a gay man at the same time, I didn't really tell many people. I was too afraid. I lived for years in fear that I could lose the kids and even my job, so I just dealt with it and kept my mouth shut.

I didn't have the confidence in myself or in others.

As I went through life, there were no other people like me. There were very few divorced or single fathers, and even fewer gay ones. I wasn't a pioneer per se, but most of the time I felt like it. With other gay people, I was often the only one who had been married to a woman, and usually the only one with kids.

If not a pioneer, I was definitely an anomaly, and I'm sure many thought I was a freak.

Best case, I was a curiosity that sparked a million questions. Nothing came easy, and nothing came without a struggle. I tried my best to protect my kids from it all, which meant constant compromising to keep the peace.

When I found love, it got much better but then he had his own issues to handle, suddenly thrust into a relationship with kids. He went in knowingly and happily, but who could really know what would be in store?

While the times have changed, many of the emotions that we all experience have not changed at all.

We all still struggle in our own way, and many of the thoughts and feelings that I experienced are still the same today, despite the different circumstances. We still experience prejudice, we still fear being held back at work, and we still find it hard to make friends.

No matter who we are.

And no matter what people say, it's still hard to tell someone that you're gay, or that your dad is gay.

I don't want my children to feel any of that, but I know I can't shield them from it. But I can help give them the confidence to deal with it all, with pride.

People ask me now how I can possibly do it all: run an agency, blog every day, write books, teach classes, sit on boards. The truth is that this is puppy chow compared to the days when the kids were young. THAT was exhausting and unsustainable. This is nothing, absolutely nothing.

I have the confidence to do anything now.

I want my children to have that same confidence. It's my duty, and it's my gift.

I can say with 100% confidence that I have tried to prepare them…

CHAPTER 31
Next Generation

It hit me the other day just how hard it must be on the kids, perhaps *even more so* now.

I don't mean to sound like I've been insensitive all of these years. Quite the contrary, my biggest fear was that they would suffer because of their dad. I worried that somehow, because of the life I led and who I am, they would bear the brunt of prejudice.

Despite trying my hardest, I know they faced criticism and prejudice, just like I did growing up. Just like any of us do growing up. The truth is that prejudice does not discriminate. Everyone faces judgment and everyone gets criticized at some point.

Everyone has *something* that makes them different.

We are all a "minority" in some manner. It might be color, a particular challenge, a size or shape, gender…we all have something that sets us apart and that others could use against us if they so choose. It's just a matter of how we each deal with our differences, and what we each make of them.

I've certainly faced my fair share, but I've never been one to complain about it or let it hold me back. While it may bother me right then and there, I put my head down and plow ahead. I try not to let it affect me or slow me down in the long run.

I just hope that the kids can adopt the same attitude as they hit adult milestones now. I still worry…I'm their dad. I worry that they will face the same issues that I faced, because of me.

How can I expect them to endure the questions that once haunted me? I am sure it happens, on a daily basis, especially when they are out and about meeting new people.

"Your father's gay?"

"What was it like to have a gay father?"

"Did your friends make fun of you because your father was gay?"

"Were your mother and father married?"

"Did Christopher break up their marriage?"

It's endless, I am sure.

Despite the fact that the kids never tell me, I know they face these questions and I know it has to bother them. I'm sure some situations are worse than others.

I heard that my daughter had faced a barrage of questions when she first went to high school. You remember what it's like to start at a new school: questions fly around and rumors run rampant. Well then imagine a Catholic high school and one of the new freshmen has a gay father. The horror!

Well, evidently the gossip got so bad that my daughter decided she had to confront it. She identified one of the ringleaders behind the gossip, I'm not sure how, and marched right up to her. "I hear you have some questions about me," she poked at the girl. "Feel free to ask me to my face and I'll be happy to tell you."

Wow!

Reminds me of when she had her hair chopped off and I was the only one worried about what her friends would say. You go, girl! (Hope I didn't date myself too much with that comment).

One day I remember my son came home from elementary school very upset. He was totally out of sorts, so much so that even Christopher couldn't break through to him. I knew there was something really wrong, so I kept at him.

Through a lot of tears, I finally got him to admit that someone said to him, "Your dad's a faggot." There's the "f" word I'd been dreading. There's the bullying I'd been dreading. There's the moment I'd been dreading.

I tried to calm him down; I tried to reason with him. All he kept saying through the tears was, "But he doesn't know you." Exactly. Just like my daughter, wise beyond his years.

So my kids have some confidence, more than I ever had when I was their age. But I still worried. I worried about how they would feel when they went to college for the first time and had to tell their roommates and every single new friend about their family.

Both kids had full time jobs this summer…did their bosses ask about their family?

I still worry that they get the endless barrage of questions that I used to get. Questions that I couldn't handle confidently, but I'm hoping they feel differently about.

I'd like to think that my fears are unfounded. I'd like to think that times have changed enough since I was going through it that they don't need to deal with it. I'd like to think that we've really changed as a society. Our friends tell us not to worry, and there certainly are signs that we can start to relax.

I marvel at how involved fathers are now in their children's lives. I am so happy to see the stores, streets, schools, and parks filled with men. I soak in every story I hear from my team at work about how the dads are taking paternity leave and how they are accompanying their wives to doctor visits and teacher conferences. I love seeing every brand that features an active dad in their marketing, and now there are a lot of them.

Just the other day on the subway in New York, I saw a dad dressed in a suit for work with his arm around the chest of his young son who was wearing a school uniform. It was obvious that it was the first day of school and that the son was a bit apprehensive. The dad kept kissing his son on the top of his head as he stared into space. All I could think about was when I was in that same situation with my son.

As men we've evolved, and as a society dads have become much more accepted as caregivers in the family, no matter the makeup of the family.

Groups of dads get together now to share stories and to support each other, just as much as groups of moms do. Just browse through a few Twitter hash tags and you'll see communities of fathers banding together.

When I dropped my son off at college this year, there was a big banner that instructed students to do three things before the end of the day: "Complete Fall Registration, Buy Books, Call Your Dad."

I never would have seen that when I was in college.

Facebook has become a source of joy for me. My Facebook feed is filled with pictures of friends' children who are advancing through school, applying to college, graduating, and getting jobs. I smile from ear to ear when I see men announce "We're getting married" or "Just married" on their posts. I see colleagues that I've worked with through the years, gay men younger than me, posting birth announcements and baby photos on Facebook.

Mainstream brands are featuring same sex couples and gay dads on a more regular basis. Even brands like Banana Republic and Tiffany are out.

I literally never thought I'd see the day.

YouTube is loaded with viral videos of dads who have captured hysterical footage while caring for their kids. I watch as many as I can; some make me laugh and some make me cry. The really good ones do both!

I witnessed firsthand the rise of the Daddy Blogger at work. As social media started to explode, moms started exercising their voice through blogging. It was a breakthrough time in our culture as "real" people became influential in marketing and branding. Not long after, the dads took their turn at the keyboard and started exercising their voice as bloggers and parents as well. In just a few short years, the Daddy Bloggers have become a force. I guess in a way, I'm one of them too. I never thought about it that way before, but here I am!

Deep in my heart, I know that the questions my kids now face are ones of curiosity, not of judgment. Curiosity is okay if it's about learning and exploring and embracing everything that makes us all different. I'm all for that.

When one of my son's friends sincerely and legitimately asked me how I met Christopher, I almost fell out of my chair.. I couldn't answer him. I was speechless. I walked into the bathroom with my eyes full of tears. I cried because he really wanted to know. I'm crying now writing about it.

Maybe I don't have to fear those questions as much.

Thankfully, the world's a different place now. It's a place where gay people are more generally accepted, and even sometimes assumed, particularly in places where I have chosen to live. Gay marriage (something not even dreamed of when I came out) is now legal in twenty-six states (and counting) and also in nineteen countries (and counting) around the world.

Babies are being born into gay households at the same rate as straight households, and at an even higher rate when the gay couple is married. The census data proves it. Schools have programs to help children thrive no matter who they are and no matter who their parents are.

Pop culture standouts are helping to move the cause forward. Macklemore and Ryan Lewis gained immense popularity for their song *Same Love*, calling out all gay prejudice as pure hatred, just like any other kind of prejudice, hoping to inspire equality.

Marketing, advertising, social media, and of course Hollywood have such profound effect on our cultural perceptions and acceptances. It shapes it and also reflects it. I've seen that on both sides now.

We now live in a world where young gay people finally have role models that they can look to and say, "Hey, that's me." We watch televisions shows, go to the movies, and listen to music that accurately portrays gay people in a very positive way.

There is now a range of specific support groups and organizations whose sole purpose is to help the various flavors of the LGBT community and their families.

If only I had then what others have now. I am so happy to see it.

I've looked at life from both sides now.

We sold the last house we all lived in, the one where the kids spent all their high school years and part of college. Sniff, sniff. We are ready to move on to our next chapter in life, just as the kids are moving onto theirs.

The night before the kids went back to college from a long, wonderful summer, we celebrated our last night together in the house. We all knew what we were doing, but we didn't really acknowledge it. I personally couldn't because I would have been crying the whole time. Christopher was fighting back tears enough as it was; I couldn't fuel the fire.

We just spent the night together, just being us, nothing special at all. We had our universal favorite for dinner, Cincinnati Chili, to say goodbye, and of course artichoke dip. Well, not goodbye, but you know what I mean.

The next day, Sophie sat in the garage, in her usual stance, watching us go back and forth as we packed the kids' cars. She knew what was happening too. I hear people say all the time, "Where does the time go?" Now I know what they mean.

In many ways, I'd like to think we are all the better for dealing with our struggles and learning from them. I'd like to think we are better people as a result. I'd like to think that we've prepared the children for their future. I give their mom credit for it too.

The glass is now full.

Truth be told, it's not about being a dad or a mom or anything in between… it's about being a loving parental figure in any way, shape, or form that it takes. It's all about love, whatever the form.

As a father, "husband," and businessman, I've lived a life of love and happiness, and I hope and think that my children are confident about where they've come from, all parts of it.

Nothing has made me happier than being an *Out and About Dad*. I am the luckiest man on the earth to have been living the life I've shared with my family. I wouldn't trade it for the world, none of it. I am happy and proud of all that we've done together, and look forward to so much more.

I present this book in tribute to the lives we have lived, together, and to the advances in our culture. I hope this book helps others to be happy and proud too. Here's to the next generation!

NYC DADS GROUP

During the process of writing this book, my friend Gwen introduced me to one of the founders of the NYC Dads Group, Lance Somerfeld. @NYCDadsGroup.

Lance and his friend Matt Schneider formed the group when they both became dads and realized that they could use some support. They started out slowly…a meetup here and there where a few other dads would join them for an activity with their kids. These small meetups turned into bigger gatherings, some sponsored by brands looking to present their products as a help to these dads.

The NYC Dads Group has now grown to numerous cities around the country. @SFDadsGroup, @ATLDadsGroup, @DenverDadsGroup, etc., etc.

When Gwen first turned me onto the group, I got excited about their Facebook activity and Twitter feeds but it wasn't until I went to a meetup myself that I experienced the power of the NYC Dads Group.

I have never seen so many engaged fathers in one place in my life! Sure there were a bunch of stay-at-home dads (#SAHD), but there were also dads from every walk of life – every form and every flavor – married, divorced, widowed, single. I'm sure there was even a #SGD or two.

They have a hashtag that joins them together.

The topic of this meetup was car seat safety, and the guys were soaking in the information like their lives depended on it. Actually, like their kids' lives depended on it. A couple of *Buds* and a slice or two of pizza later, and the night was complete.

I sat in amazement because I couldn't help but think what my life, and my kids' lives, would have been like if we had such a support group to join and to lean on. My attitudes and behaviors would have been completely different, and I'm certain I would have relaxed a whole lot more.

I didn't have a hashtag to join.

It brings me great joy to know that these support groups now exist and I stand in awe of two gentlemen like Lance and Matt who made it happen.

Bravo!

OUT AND ABOUT DAD
Playlist

Greatest Love Of All, Whitney Houston
MacArthur Park, Donna Summer
Vogue, Madonna
Waterfalls, TLC
One by One, Cher
Part Of Your World, from *The Little Mermaid*
Someone Like You, Linda Eder
Dancing with Myself, Billy Idol
Hot Stuff, Donna Summer
Desperado, Linda Ronstadt
Last Dance, Donna Summer
Eminence Front, The Who
Under My Thumb, The Rolling Stones
I Am What I Am, Gloria Gaynor
I Will Survive, Gloria Gaynor
Knock On Wood, Amii Stewart
The Wind Beneath My Wings, Bette Midler
You Light Up My life, Debbie Boone
You're My Best Friend, Queen
1812 Overture, The Colonial Williamsburg Fifes and Drums
The Way We Were, Barbra Streisand
Edge of Glory, Lady Gaga
Same Love, Macklemore and Ryan Lewis
Both Sides Now, Joni Mitchell
What Are You Doing The Rest of Your Life, Frank Sinatra

For inspiration back in the day and again now writing this book:
Breakaway, Donna Summer

Forget about the bad times
Remember all the good times
Hold your head up high

MWAH!

A heartfelt thank you to my dream team
who helped me bring my story to life:

Jeremy Baka
Martin Fitzpatrick
Karen Greishaber, etc., etc., etc.
Alicia Joseph
JP Joseph
Gwen Korbel
Stephanie Slatt
Lance Somerfeld
Helayne Spivak
Christopher Warns

And all my friends at Mascot Books,
especially Naren Aryal and Laura Carroll

IN DEDICATION

I dedicate this book to Christopher.

We jumped into each other's lives so very long ago, not really knowing where our journey would take us.

I am not me without you.

What are you doing the rest of your life?
North and South and East and West of your life.

IN MEMORIAM

FOREVER SOPHIE

The Baroness Miss Sophie Delight
December 2002 – October 2014